Friends, for Life

The Psychology of Close Relationships

Friends, for Life

The Psychology of Close Relationships

Steve Duck

Senior Lecturer in Psychology
University of Lancaster

ST. MARTIN'S PRESS
New York

© Steve Duck 1983

St. Martin's Press, Inc., 175 Fifth Avenue, New York, NY 10010
Printed in Great Britain
First published in the United States of America in 1983

ISBN 0-312-30564-8

Library of Congress Cataloging in Publication Data

Duck, Steve.
  Friends, for life.

  1. Friendship.   2. Intimacy (Psychology)   I. Title.
BF575.F66D83   1983   158'.25   82-25081
ISBN 0-312-30564-8

Contents

11954

For
Sandra, Christina, Jamie,
Robin,
and the rest of my 5.6

Acknowledgements

Several people contributed in knowing and unknowing ways to the completion of this book. Some of them gave me insights that stemmed from things they had said or stories that they told me; some of them read and commented on the manuscript as I was writing and polishing it. In particular I would like to acknowledge the enormous debt that I owe my father, Kenneth W. Duck, not only for the great care and conscientiousness with which he read the manuscript and for the many invaluable improvements that he suggested but for incalculable other contributions over the years which helped to make it possible for me to write this book.

1

Our Friends, Ourselves

In both the USA and the UK broken marriages are increasing at a rate so alarming that it now takes thousands of dollars and thousands of pounds every minute to pay for the costs[1]. In other words each US citizen — man, woman and child — pays a dollar a day (and every single UK citizen pays 50p daily) to foot the bill for other people's failed marriages. This hidden relationship tax is on top of the price for looking after disrupted families and broken homes. It is in addition to what we pay when unpopular children grow into adult violent criminals or develop mental illness. It is extra to the cost of industrial disputes between people who cannot get on together at work. Perhaps more significantly, to count such costs only in monetary terms is to take no account of the human waste and misery that result from poor relationships. Researchers have now established that friendship problems go hand in hand with many different social problems such as alcoholism, violence and suicide. It is also found that unpopularity in childhood foreshadows many difficulties in later life, such as delinquency and career misadventures. More than this, it appears that people with poor relationships are prone to many other misfortunes — some of which are directly caused by the worry of stress in their relationships, and some of which are startling curiosities that just seem to go along with unsatisfactory friendships. For example, it is beginning to be realised that, for some reason, people with fewer friends are more prone to tonsillitis and cancer; while people who are in the process of divorcing actually stand an increased risk of heart disease, injury in traffic accidents, and being attacked by muggers. As final examples, people who are poor at making friends have been shown to have worse teeth and to get more serious illnesses (Lynch, 1977; Bloom *et al.*, 1978).

These consequences afflict more people than we may think, and indeed in other ways they can affect us all, since we are all called from time to time to help friends in distress or in difficulties with their relationships. Everyone goes through difficulties in their friendships, most of us lose friends we would have liked to keep, and all of us see relationships going sour and becoming unsatisfying from time to time. Surprisingly, even in such apparently minor cases the research indicates beyond a shadow of a doubt that we are putting our physical and psychological health at risk. Some researchers are starting to claim a direct connection between friendship problems and breakdown of the body's defences against invasion by viruses (Lynch, 1977). So it is not merely for reasons of enjoyment and satisfaction that we need to keep our friendships in good repair and try to let them help us; we need friends for life: to make us — and keep us — whole. Given this, it is important that we do start and manage friendships properly, yet the above figures suggest that a lot of people do not. Assuredly, when left to their own devices most people would get by most of the time, but still fail to maximise their potential in friendship. But after all, using their own devices is what most people have had to do so far — including the growing numbers who get divorced.

So it would be foolish to deny that the more we can find out about our own friendships, the better we can surround ourselves with the human medical insurance and the social support that act as important safeguards against occupational stress, psychological illness, negative life events, and the like. The more we learn about the origins and causes of relational success and failure, the better we can deal with such personal questions as: How can we predict or increase our marital satisfaction? and how can we increase the chances of our children maturing into stable, sociable, healthy adults? We would also learn more about general social problems, such as how to prevent distressful interaction in disturbed families, how to reduce disruption in classrooms, and how to create effective and co-operative work and sales teams. These and a host of other issues that directly affect all our daily lives are the practical consequences of thinking hard about friendship.

8

Unfortunately, when some people think about these questions they focus on the wrong answers, or turn to the wrong places for advice. There are many people who still cherish the belief that relationships and friendships between human beings are nothing more than a matter of common sense — even when their own relationships go sour. Yet if we only look to common sense for answers, or read popular magazine problem pages, and consult palmists or the tea leaves, then we are in for some nasty shocks and some misleading advice. In any case, we have had common sense — along with these other 'experts' — for a very long time: all the time that the divorce rate has been climbing so dramatically in fact. Common sense has failed us and so have these so-called experts. For this reason it is only recently that systematic research on personal relationships has started to grow, as more and more people have begun to recognise the inadequacy of intuition and common sense in such an important area of all our lives. The researchers encompass a wide range of disciplines, and include psychiatrists, medical researchers, social psychologists, child psychologists, ethologists, marriage counsellors, and criminologists (see Duck and Gilmour 1981 a, b, c: Duck, 1982).

In looking at the growing number of scientific studies of friendship and personal relationships, this book tries to sort out the commonsense truth from the commonsense nonsense, the myth with a grain of insight from the belief that is demonstrably unfounded or simply false. Many such beliefs exist because friendship feels commonsensical and appears to be misleadingly natural and easy when it is going well. It isn't something that we are used to concentrating on or experimenting with.

Yet this misleading feeling disguises from us the harder truth that it is actually a very complicated and prolonged process with many pitfalls and challenges. Friendships do not just happen; they have to be made — made to start, made to work, made to develop, kept in good working order, and preserved from going sour. To do all this we need to be active and we need to be skilful. Indeed, to suggest that you just start a friendship and off it goes is as simple-minded as believing that you drive down the motorway just by turning the ignition key, then sitting back and letting the journey take care of itself. On the contrary, much careful adjustment and continuous monitoring is

9

required, along with several very sophisticated skills (Trower, *et al.*, 1978). To develop a close friendship with someone who used to be a stranger we have to assess the other person accurately, adopt appropriate styles of communication and bodily posture, and find out how to satisfy mutual personality needs; we have to learn to adjust our behaviour to the other person and to select and reveal the right sorts of information or opinions in an inviting, encouraging way in the appropriate style and circumstances; we have to build up trust, to make suitable demands and build up commitment; and we have to perform all the other more difficult skills that the remaining chapters here discuss more fully. In brief, these necessitate proficiency in presenting ourselves efficiently, attending to the right features of the other person at the right time, and pacing the friendship properly. Rather like learning to drive a car, we have to pick up these different abilities and co-ordinate them, and just as when we have learned to drive we need to concentrate harder each time we get into a new model, so with unfamiliar relationships we have to relearn, modify or focus more carefully on the things that we do. All of us have pet stories about the strain, embarrassment and awkwardness that occurred in a first meeting with a new neighbour or a friend of a friend: some clumsy silence, an ill-judged phrase, a difficult situation. It is in such situations that the skills of friendship are bared and tested to the limits, and where intuition is most often not enough. Mistakes, misperceptions, miscommunications, solecisms, and gaffes are all too easy, and all too final. Yet because it is a skill, friendship — even for these situations — is something that can be improved, coached and practised like any other skill, trained like any other, and made more fluent.

Since we are not usually disposed to think of friendship and close relationships in this new kind of way, people usually feel irrationally resistant to doing so. We tend not to conceptualise friendship as something that needs to be concentrated on, developed and thought about in the way that the research shows to be useful. We are happy to see it merely as a pleasant, passive state: it just happens to us and we don't have to do anything particular — let alone do anything properly, except appear friendly. This could not be further from the truth, and all respectable research scholars in the field now regard friendship as a *process* that continues right through the life of the relationship, with a constant and perpetual need for the right actions and activities at the right time to keep it all alive (Hinde, 1979; Morton and Douglas, 1981).

This book takes a close look at such research and looks at the system that is friendship development. I shall explore the general styles and detailed behaviours that are essential to constructive and satisfying friendship, the differences that characterise successful and unsuccessful styles in friendship, dating and marriage, and the errors that are most often made in creating relationships.

One advantage of this way of looking at friendship is obvious: it leads to a direct and useful form of practical advice for people who are unhappy with one or more of their relationships, or who are lonely or frustrated. It focuses us on what people can *do* to improve their relationships, and takes away the tendency to be resigned about it, or worse to blame, namecall, stigmatise or mock and deride people who are lonely or friendless. It stops us swallowing the 'Identi-friend' theory proposed by common sense — that we start out either attractive or unattractive and need only change our possessions or our physical characteristics to become attractive, the theory so beloved of the deodorant and vermouth advertising-machines. The new approach adopted here will stop us believing that people with few friends are not selected because they are just socially valueless: it focuses us on what these people do wrong at the various stages of friendship development and how it can be corrected. People who have no friends are not social and personal failures; they are probably just not performing the behaviours of friendship in a properly polished manner. It isn't that they possess some magic anti-charm; it is not a fixed attribute, but something that they can learn to change, once they can shake off the outmoded ideas of common sense and accept the idea that friendship can be practised and experimented on.

Is it such a strange and unacceptable idea that people can be trained to adopt more satisfactory styles in relationships? Not really. We are all familiar with the fact that doctors and dentists receive instruction on how to establish rapport with other people, and how to develop a reassuring and constructive 'bedside manner'. We also know that insurance salesmen are trained in how to relate to possible customers, that airline hostesses receive instruction on relating to passengers, and that personnel managers spend a lot of time trying to establish good personal relationships with staff. These people receive extra training to make them into sociable experts, the rest of us usually don't. We are left to our own devices, for the most part, and we are expected to pick up the knowledge informally, perhaps during schooldays or at play, or from the hard knocks that life gives us when we get it wrong. These experiences are supposed to be all that we need to teach us how to treat other people, and for a lot of us they are barely adequate most of the time. Although they are utterly unstructured and completely unsystematic, they serve as reasonable guides for most of the relationships we shall get into. But what we shall never know, if we rely on this alone, is whether our relationships will be as broad and satisfying as they might be, could be, or should be.

The evidence suggests that all of us are probably missing out and not maximising our potential for friendships. American research (Reisman, 1981) shows that people claim to have about fifteen friends on average, although the numbers change with age (17-year olds claim about nineteen, whilst 28-year olds have only twelve; 45-year olds have acquired sixteen, while people in their sixties enjoy an average of fifteen). When people are asked to name the relationships that are satisfying, intimate and close, however, the number drops dramatically to around six (5·6 to be precise!). Obviously, people don't get the maximum satisfaction that they could achieve and would benefit from some guidance about the ways to make friendships more satisfying. We are, perhaps, used to thinking of only the lonely people needing to improve their friendships. Surely, they are the ones who express their dissatisfaction most often and write to advice columnists because their misery becomes unbearable. But when they do, out comes the trite and useless advice: 'Join clubs and meet more people.' But if someone is lonely or friendless because they are doing friendship wrongly, then telling them to join clubs and meet people is as valueless and unhelpful as giving a monkey a piano and telling it to play 'The Flight of the Bumblebee'. In both cases they have the right equipment, but do not know how to use it properly. To a lesser extent this may be true of everyone who feels dissatisfied or unfulfilled by their relationships. Everyone wants to know if their friendships are as numerous and varied as they should be, and most people usually suspect that things can be improved.

To begin to answer the questions of how relationships can be improved and made more satisfying, it is instructive to look at what it is that we lack when friendships go wrong. Whatever it is, it is so disorienting and disturbing that it must obviously be something fundamental to human experience. What do we need friends for, and what do we lose when we experience disruption of friendship?

Why We Need Friends

There are several ways to start answering the large question about why we need friends. One way is to examine what happens to people who deliberately cut themselves off from their friends or who take jobs that effectively do it for them — people like hermits, Arctic explorers, religious ascetics, and lighthouse keepers. After all, if they have made an informed and calculated decision to go into a form of isolation, we would expect the effect to be less extreme because they will already have foreseen, evaluated and taken it into account. As expected, it is found (Schachter, 1959) that such people are usually quite well prepared to suffer the effects of their decision. Many ascetic religious orders explicitly train novices by enforcing periods of silence even when they still meet other novices, or they isolate them for short periods before restricting them totally, and in this way they gradually prepare them for what is to come. In time, at any rate, they are less seriously affected by their isolation than are people who have had loneliness thrust upon them without any choice, or who did not realise what they were letting themselves in for. For instance, I have had long conversations with drivers of one-man-operated buses who hanker after the time in the cafeteria when they can meet their mates, or who really don't resent the difficult passenger who needs to be dealt with in a close encounter! Some of my students have reported the same sort of experience as many other bedsitters when they are moved from a campus residential block out into bedsit-land in their second year. The first hour or so of each day is spent finding friends to communicate with and talk to after they have commuted from their flat to their workplace.

These are much less serious (though more familiar) than the very extreme reactions that researchers have found when studying the period of adjustment to total voluntary isolation (Schachter, 1959). Hermits and recluses often write that they have had dreams about groups of people or about being in a crowd or meeting friends. They also report spending a lot of the time daydreaming about other people. In extreme cases, it is found that hermits have the hallucination that other people are present, speaking to them. Tests have shown that such hallucinations are not simply due to some psychological abnormality like schizophrenia, but rather they seem to show an exaggerated normal response. Bereaved persons or isolated prisoners sometimes report the same sort of feelings. Many people who lose a lifelong companion, spouse or close friend report feeling as if their dead partner is present in the room with them, or speaks softly to them, or is just there, watching over them. This familiar response to grief is so well known and so general that we can safely say that it tells us something crucial about the human need for companionship. Yet it does not tell us why we need friends, it merely shows us one of the ways in which the human mind protects itself when friends and companions are lost — by manufacturing them for us! This in itself is a finding that should prepare us to expect some rather unusual effects of friendship upon the human mind.

Some people are doing no more than respond to social pressures when they become recluses: their behaviour may be so odd or unacceptable that becoming a recluse is one rational way to escape the scorn and mockery of other people. Some individuals become recluses through fear of the hygienic consequences of meeting people — Howard Hughes, for example, the multi-millionaire, built an elaborate castle of defences around himself because he became afraid of catching germs and diseases from other people. Such people have often weighed up the likely consequences and advantages of their isolation before they embark upon it and so they have, to that extent, discounted, allowed for, and even actively sought, the effects that their isolation will bring.

Although people like that are not typical cases, they do make one important point: isolation and aloneness are different from loneliness. Loneliness is a *feeling* about isolation, and people can be isolated without feeling lonely just as they can feel lonely without being isolated. Isolation is physical separation from other people, but loneliness is the feeling that you do not have as many friends, or the sort of friends, that you wish you had, or enough of the opportunities to meet them that you desire.

1 A sense of belonging

For this reason, isolation creates feelings of loneliness most severely in people who have not chosen it personally (e.g. those who are put in solitary confinement) or have not anticipated it (e.g. those who are bereaved unexpectedly) or have it happen to them in less extreme forms — for instance, when people go into hospital they often experience loneliness although they are surrounded by helpful people. This feeling of loneliness could be due to many things: the separation from loved ones, the sudden immersion in a new environment, or the anxieties of being a patient causing them to need reassurance that friends could provide. However, one surprising factor emerges as more important. It is the fact that they lose the sense of belonging. There are two reasons: first, they now become passive and visits have to be scheduled by someone else; secondly, there are 'belonging limits' placed on conversation, since it turns inwards, or it centres on reports of what is happening outside — where the patient is excluded from going.

This sort of loneliness will not be lightly dismissed by caring hospital staff, as it has been shown that it leads to a lower resistance to disease and a slower rate of recovery. It can affect a patient's spirits enough to affect the will to fight the disease: investigators now know that patients with a terminal illness die sooner if they have only a small group of friends than if they are popular and have a happy, supportive family. Interestingly, insurance companies have not yet seen the implications of this for their actuarial prediction of life-expectancy. Yet it is conclusively and repeatedly shown that lonely people die younger, and more often risk death through serious illness (Lynch, 1977; Bloom *et al.*, 1978; Perlman and Peplau, 1981).

Another area where loneliness can have serious effects because friendship research was ignored is in the now infamous

15

tower-block residences. Not knowing about friendship research, planners did not foresee the full consequences of these social monstrosities, and failed to predict the relationship problems they would create. Yet friendship researchers could point to research going back thirty years that predicted precisely the outcomes that are now being experienced such as alienation, depression and violence. Indeed, a major effort of such researchers in the late 1940s was directed at the context provided by the layout of housing accommodation for the social relationships in the community (Festinger *et al.*, 1950). What is important is not just how physically close the houses are on an estate, nor how small the flats are in a tower block, but how the front doors of the houses and flats are positioned: even people who live next door to one another will be less friendly if their front doors face the same way rather than facing each other. Neighbours stand more chance of becoming friends if their front doors face one another, even if their houses are a bit further away than from a house with a front door facing the same way. Other findings from the same research programme show that the important thing in such design is not the physical arrangement, but the 'psychological arrangement' of the accommodation. Alas, planners heard about the work too late. (Now, incidentally, researchers are predicting some unforeseen consequences of unemployment, building design and the school system which I shall stress later.)

The consequences of loneliness in these circumstances will be disregarded only by the uncaring and shortsighted. We must not assume, because the less extreme effects of loneliness are more familiar, that those mild effects are all that there are. We all know that people in hospitals or people who move house to an unfamiliar neighbourhood experience boredom and loneliness, but few of us have realised that the effects can be vastly more serious. Loneliness is fatal. Bereaved spouses die more shortly after the death of their partner than would be predicted from statistical evidence about life-expectancy (Lynch, 1977; Bloom *et al.*, 1978), and 'death of a spouse' yields one of the highest scores for the widow(er)'s 'dangerous life events' score. It is not surprising then, that the time of bereavement is precisely one where our culture requires that our friends rally round, make more effort to exercise their friendship, call round more often, and offer help and a sense of community or belonging. These apparently inconsequential activities are actually ways of helping to stave off the most severe consequences of loneliness, such as depression, illness and death. The trick is learning how to entice others to perform these activities for us.

2 Emotional integration and stability

Importantly, communities provide a lot more for people than just a sense of belonging (Weiss, 1974). They also provide necessary anchor points for opinions, beliefs and emotional responses: they tell us how we should react, and they correct or guide our attitudes and beliefs in subtle ways. For instance, we all know that different cultures react differently to grief: in some countries it is acceptable to fall to the ground, cover oneself with dust and wail loudly when one is bereaved; in other cultures it is completely unacceptable to show such emotion, and the emphasis falls on dignified public composure. Imagine the reaction in Britain if the Queen were to exhibit the former way of demonstrating grief, or if Jackie Kennedy had decided that the proper way to attend her husband's funeral was wearing a party dress and a broad grin! Humans have available many different ways of demonstrating grief, but they are supposed to cope with this strong emotion in a way particularly acceptable to their own culture. In short, the appropriate way of showing it is defined, endorsed and encouraged by the particular community in which the individuals find themselves. Equally, the strong cultural pressure lasts throughout one's life and it is not the case that, in a matter like this, one behaves as the Romans do when in Rome. One's *psychological* community influences the way one reacts.

Friends as well as cultures develop their own sets of shared concerns, common interests and collective problems, as well as shared meanings, common responses to life and communal emotionality. Friends are often appreciated exactly because they share these private understandings, private jokes or private language. To be sure, these are much more localised than those beliefs that are shared by everyone in a particular country or culture, but for that reason they are more important in daily life. Indeed, daily life is built round them and loneliness or isolation is important psychologically precisely because it

17

deprives people of their psychological bench-marks and anchor points: they lose the stability provided by the chance to compare their own reactions to life with the reactions of other people that they know, like and respect.

This is important for a number of reasons. First of all, it is well established that responses to almost anything can be markedly influenced by other folk's reactions. For instance, a classic finding of social psychology (Sherif, 1936) is that people will believe that they see a stationary light moving if they are placed in a group that consistently claims to see the light move. They can even be induced to offer very precise measurements of the distance that it moved.

Friends provide a stable, meaningful background for responses to many less spectacular and more familiar things such as political events, other people, work, the weather and life. If these stabilities and comparisons are taken away from someone, they become uncertain and unstable. This fact has been used by experienced 'brain-washers' whose cardinal rule is to separate prisoners from groups of familiar companions and place them in isolation or, perhaps, force them to join groups of alien prisoners to whom they cannot easily communicate and check their beliefs, feelings or responses. Such experiences are intentionally disruptive and often require great efforts of will by the prisoner to overcome. Isolation and solitary confinement in such conditions can play havoc with people's sanity — and they are intended to do so in these circumstances. Nowadays the powerful punishing effects of enforced isolation are recognised in both military and civil prisons. Solitary confinements or removal of association rights are both used as formal punishments in civil prisons, and would not be so unless they were recognised to be disturbing and unpleasant. Who would give someone solitary confinement as a punishment if they knew that the person merely saw it as a welcome opportunity for some peace and quiet?

Not many people realise that it is a very mild version of this form of disorientation that is experienced when they go on holidays to other countries, or when executives cross the Atlantic and feel 'culture shock'. It can be unbalancing to be confronted with a completely unfamiliar range of beliefs, systems, styles and habits: that, after all, is one of the problems that we try to avoid

18

precisely by creating a stable and familiar group of friends at home. It seems to be the case that the disorientation is reduced when we travel with people that we like, or when we meet close friends at the other end. Business travellers who are met by disliked or unfamiliar colleagues are actually likely to be more uncomfortable, disoriented and ineffective in adjusting to the new environment, although companies who pay enormous sums to transfer executives across the Atlantic are surprisingly inattentive to this small point, so easily corrected.

So loneliness and isolation are also disruptive because they deprive the person of the opportunity for comfortable comparison of opinions and attitudes with other people — close friends. The persons become anxious, disoriented, unhappy, and even severely destabilised emotionally. This 'stokes itself' on some occasions and they may become even more anxious just because they feel themselves behaving erratically, or they experience unusual mood swings. They often report sudden changes of temper and loss of control, sometimes resulting in violent outbursts; but in any case their judgment becomes erratic and unreliable, and they may become unusually vigilant, suspicious or jumpy in the presence of other unfamiliar people.

Another function of friendship, then, another reason why we need friends, is to keep us emotionally stable and to help us see where we stand *vis-à-vis* other people and whether we are 'doing OK'. It is particularly noticeable in times of stress and crisis. I particularly remember an occasion when all the lights fused in a residence block. The rational thing to do was to find a flashlight and await the restoration of power. What we all actually did was to stumble down to the common-room and chatter amongst ourselves: the need to compare our reactions to the emergency was so powerful and so universal, that even the warden did the same, a doctor who had been to Oxford *and* Cambridge! But this often happens after any kind of stress or crisis, right from the crowd of people who gather to swap stories and compare their responses after a fire or a car accident, to the nervous chatter that schoolchildren get involved in when the doctor comes to 'give them the needle'.

In a crisis, or during loneliness and isolation, people's confidence in their emotional stability gets shaken, causing vacillation of opinions and wobbling of the structure of thoughts and feelings in alarming ways. Small wonder that the extremes of solitary confinement and the milder forms of disorientation are so unpleasant; but there is an everyday lesson here too. Equally punishing and equally far-reaching are the effects of unintentionally self-imposed or self-created isolation or the strongly negative consequences, for a person's mental state, caused by social rejection and loneliness. And of course there are also the disabled and housebound — people who may be perfectly capable of the necessary social behaviours, but who suffer the psychological effects of isolation and loneliness for different reasons. Too often we overlook the tragic social and psychological consequences of such physical disability, and do not appreciate the extent of the psychological effects that it has been shown to have. Neither in our own lives do we necessarily attend carefully enough to the right ways of ensuring that we have a network of friends to keep us emotionally stable.

3 Opportunities for communication about ourselves

If we look even further into it, however, we find more reasons why we need friends (Weiss, 1974). One centrally important one is communication. This particular wheel was strikingly re-invented by the Quaker prison reformers several generations ago, who attempted to cut down communication between prisoners in order to stop them educating one another about ways of committing crime. Accordingly, one of their proposals was that prisoners should be isolated from one another. What occurred was very instructive: the prisoners spent most of their time tapping out coded messages on walls and pipes, devising means of passing information to one another, and working out clever ways of communicating. Evidently, people who are involuntarily isolated feel a need to communicate. One additional function that healthy friendships provide, then, is a place for such communication to occur — communication about all sorts of things, not only general events or circumstances but also personal, intimate details about oneself.

A mild form of this overbrimming need to communicate is to be found on railway trains. Here many lonely people strike up conversations — but usually monologues — which allow them to communicate to someone or to tell someone about themselves and their opinions. A striking thing about this is the intimacy of the stories that are often told in these circumstances. Perfect strangers can often be regaled with life histories, family details, and the personal opinions of someone they have not seen before and will probably never see again. Indeed, this is probably a key part of it, for the listener who will not be seen again cannot divulge the 'confession' to friends or colleagues and so damage the confessor's reputation. (In cases where the listener and confessor will meet again, as in the case of doctors and patients, priests and parishioners, counsellors and clients, or lawyers and consultants, the listeners are bound by strict professional ethical codes not to reveal what they have been told. On the train, the 'ethics' are simply left to statistical chance and the extreme improbability of the two strangers meeting one another's friends is a comfort in itself.) Confessions on the train also have one other notable feature: the conversation is often 'paced' to coincide with the end of the journey: the person reveals all that they want to in the course of the expected length of the journey, and unexpected delays near the end often seem to be the only thing that embarrasses them!

Another example of this same tendency occurs in hospitals. New arrivals communicate feverishly about their medical histories and symptoms, sharing their anxieties with other patients, cleaners, and maintenance staff. This is due, in part, to a need for reassurance about their condition, as well as, in part, to the general shake-down that occurs in strange surroundings. It is also a kind of magical exorcism of one's fear and anxiety about the physical complaint, a desire to communicate one's worth and importance, and to stress what will be lost if one dies.

Such examples illustrate the importance of communication, of an audience for self-expression, and the significance of opportunities to reveal 'private' details about oneself, to have someone show an interest in oneself and one's problems. Loss of such opportunities is one of the more significant consequences of social isolation, and doctors often realise that some elderly patients visit surgeries only to produce an opportunity to talk to someone. I myself have sometimes noticed that elderly patients give up their place in the queue in order to extend their conversation with someone in the waiting-room. I have even been told by some people all about their interview with the doctor — *after* they have come out. The visit was clearly not just

21

to sort out a physical problem, but to help cope with a very real psychological need. This has other less obvious forms, for instance in the case of people experiencing alienation through marital problems or through entering the early stages of divorce. They often want to find someone to 'burst' over, someone who will just listen to them as they talk themselves through the crisis. Often a good listener is all that is needed, and such people do not always need advice, they just want a sympathetic ear. Breakdown of a marriage deprives the person of communication with a (formerly) trusted listener, and so it is not surprising that this deprivation causes some of the same stressful effects as it does in other circumstances. It is particularly important, then, to ensure that we learn and keep the fullest and most effective range of communication strategies that we shall need.

4 *Provision of assistance and physical support*

A sense of belonging, emotional integration, and opportunities for communication about ourselves are only three of the reasons why we need friends. Other effects of loss of friends take different forms but, in their own ways, each wreaks a different form of psychological havoc.

For example, when people lose a friend or a spouse through bereavement, the loneliness that they report seems to be equivalent to a lack of support — they feel cut off from someone who has helped them to cope with life and to adjust to its changing uncertainties. They lose someone whose advice has been proven to be valuable or who understands them well, and can predict their moods or prevent them making mistakes and looking foolish. (A friend of mine once defined a 'friend' as someone who, seeing you drunk and about to stand up on a table and sing, would quietly take you aside to prevent you doing it.) I shall look at this woolly idea of support in more detail below, but for the moment we can simply note that it is one further need that friends fulfil: they provide us with a sense of support.

This can take one of two forms: physical support (for example, help with day-to-day tasks) and psychological support (for instance, when someone shows that we are appreciated, or lets us know that our opinions are valued). Human beings need both of these types of support, but at various times, and in various relationships one or other of them may assume a greater importance than the other. When this happens it can change the nature of the relationship (La Gaipa, 1977). This is very simply illustrated. When your friend gives you a birthday present you are supposed to accept it in a way that indicates your own unworthiness to receive it and also the kindness of the friend ('Oh you shouldn't have bothered. It really is very good of you.'). In short, you repay your friend by accepting the gift as a token of friendship and by praising the friend. You 'exchange' the gift for love and respect, as it were. Imagine what would happen if you repaid in some other way — by giving the friend the exact value of the gift in money. The friend would certainly be insulted by the ineptness: the nature of the social 'exchange' has been altered and, in so doing, you have changed the nature of the relationship.

There are other clear examples of this point that the nature of the exchange or support helps to define the degree and type of friendship. For instance, many old people get resentful of the fact that they gradually and unwillingly become more and more physically dependent on other people for help in conducting the daily business of their lives. They cannot reach things so easily, cannot look after themselves, and are more dependent physically, whilst at the same time they are less able to repay their friends by doing services in return. This, then, is one reason why many people dislike or feel uneasy with old age: they resent the feeling of helpless dependency coupled with the feeling of perpetual indebtedness that can never be paid off. At the same time the old do not feel valued *for themselves*. Gone are the days when old age was a respected time of life, and the old were held in high esteem because of their wisdom and experience. Their experience is now often felt to be outmoded, or treated as irrelevant to the changing fashions and beliefs of our time, so they can never use it as a bargaining point or 'resource' in their relationship exchange. They can't use their wisdom to 'buy' help and support as in bygone days.

People often forget that, when old people feel useless and unwanted, they are probably responding sensitively to this key fact of social life: the relationship between two people is most often defined by what the people in it provide for one another, the resources that they distribute and exchange (Chown, 1981). If I provide only services to you we are more likely to remain neighbours than become friends; if we exchange intimate secrets, it is more likely that we are close friends than strangers; if we clearly value one another's opinions and advice, share interests, and disclose our deep personal feelings, we are more likely to be thought of as friends than as enemies. A key skill that we need to develop then is an awareness of these subtle differences in exchange, and how they are used to define, contain or develop relationships.

When we put old people into the position where they receive more services than requests for advice, or more gifts than expressions of our high opinion of them, then, without even realising it, we are subtly changing the relationship from friendship to a more distant one, if not even one of 'master-servant' or 'parent-child'. Exclusively providing physical help — especially if it cannot be returned like for like — is actually a subtle and unconscious way of telling people that the relationship is not a friendship. Of course, we all do things for our friends, and these physical provisions — along with provision of assistance, information and goods — are major services that friends provide, and are very important reasons why we need friends. However, in the last analysis, all of these things can be 'purchased' by means other than friendship. Most obviously, services, information and goods can all be purchased by money or, in the case of neighbourliness, by the promise of services, information and help on a future occasion.

So we can see that friends are not, strictly, the only ones who provide us with physical support that cannot be got elsewhere — and one reason why many rich people feel friendless is precisely because they get used to buying help with money rather than by bartering their love or services in return like the rest of us do. Society very kindly labels our acts of barter as desirable and honourable ('good neighbourliness'; 'A friend in need is a friend indeed') and so we feel good when we do them. It would be difficult to conduct most of our social lives if such exchange and barter did not create the intimate chains that bind us willingly to friends. Therefore it is essential for a satisfying life that we learn and practise the hidden subtle skills of social exchange uncovered by research.

5 *Reassurance of our worth and value, and*
6 *Opportunity to help others*

We can start to explore these by looking at people who are chronically and perpetually lonely. Researchers (e.g. Perlman and Peplau, 1981) find that such people say that loss of all the above things is an important contributor to the bad way that they feel — but essentially loss of communication, help and physical support make people feel isolated without making them feel worthless. On the other hand, people who are lonely say that no one cares about them, that they are useless, uninteresting, of low value and good for nothing. Studies of suicide notes, and comments in the conversation of severely depressed people, invariably reveal indications that the people have lost their self-respect or self-esteem. In other words, they have come to see themselves as valueless, worthless and insignificant, often because that is how they feel that everyone else sees them. Indeed, scientific analysis of suicide notes shows that many suicide attempts are carried out as a way of forcing some particular friend to re-evaluate the person, or to shock them into realising just how much they really do esteem the person making the attempt. Adler once claimed, with great insight, that every suicide is always a reproach or a revenge — an attempt to show how much the person would be missed.

So, one reason that we appreciate friends is because of their contribution to our self-evaluation and esteem. Friends can do this both directly and indirectly: they may compliment us, or tell us about other people's good opinions of us — Dale Carnegie's book on how to win friends and influence people stresses the positive consequences of doing this. But they can also increase our self-esteem in other ways: by attending to what we do, listening, asking our advice and generally acting in ways that indicate the value that they place on our opinions. However, there are less obvious and more indirect ways in which they can communicate this estimation of our value. For one thing, the fact that they choose to spend time with us rather than with someone else must show that they value our company more than the alternatives.

There is a subtler version of these points too. Just as we look to our friends to provide us with all of these things, so we can get from friendship one other key benefit. Because friends trust us and depend on us they give us the chance to help *them*. That gives us the chance to take responsibility for them, to see ourselves helping them with their lives, to give them our measured advice, and consequently to feel good. Friends provide us with these opportunities for taking responsibility and 'nurturing' other people.

Undoubtedly, these things are important in the conduct of relationships and in making thm satisfactory for both partners, and it is critical that we learn to evince them effectively. However, one important point to note for later is that those people who are poor at doing what is suggested above (e.g. people who are poor at indicating interest, or who seem to have little time for other people, or never let them help or give advice) will find that other people are unattracted to relationships with them. All people need indications of their estimability and need chances to nurture just as we do, and if we do not adequately provide such signs then these people will reject us — just as we would do in their position.

So one reason why people need friends, and one of the important things that friends provide, is this sense of acceptance, of worth, of estimability. One of the consequences of isolation and social rejection is the loss of a sense of esteem, and it is not surprising that many people become severely disturbed when it is lacking. Nor is it surprising that the nature of fantasy and wish-fulfilling daydreaming in such cases is often recollection of cases where self-esteem was high (for example, past social successes or past instances where other people came for help and advice).

Perhaps it is significant in this context to note how much of our western culture is based on the idea that 'number of friends' is a good measure of social and personal success. Someone who can claim a wide network of friends is usually regarded as likely to be happy and successful. One consequence of this, by reverse logic, is that people tend to exaggerate the number of friends that they claim. This can lead to such absurdities as the claim by a well-known public performer to have sent out party invitations to 5000 of his closest and dearest personal friends!

Such ludicrous claims are mirrored to a lesser degree in all our lives in a hundred different ways and we often attempt to 'publicise' our friendships in many minor and subtle forms.

Thus, for instance, when we receive birthday cards they are not simply noted and thrown away, nor are they put in a drawer, but are displayed on window ledges or hung on walls so that they can be seen by other people and used as an unofficial — but very public — barometer of the recipient's popularity and status. The elaborate consistency of such a performance shows us something important about the reasons why we use our friendships in this way and it testifies to the joint importance of friendships in maintaining our self-esteem and of the techniques and skills that help us to bring about this support from other people.

7 Personality support

Yet there is something more fundamental to it than this. The most recent research now indicates that everything mentioned above — sense of community, emotional stability, communication, provision of help, maintenance of self-esteem, directly and indirectly — each in its own way serves to support and integrate the person's personality (Duck and Miell, 1982; Duck and Lea, 1982). Each of us is characterised by many thoughts, doubts, beliefs, attitudes, questions, hopes, expectations and opinions about the recurrent patterns that there are in life. Our personalities are composed not only of our behavioural style (for example, our introversion or extraversion) but also of our thoughts, doubts and beliefs. Our personality would fall apart if all of these opinions were not, by and large, supported. We would simply stop behaving if we had no trust in our thoughts or beliefs about why we should behave or how we should behave, just as we stop doing other things that we are convinced are wrong. Some schizophrenics actually do stop behaving when their thought-world falls apart: they just sit and stare.

Each of us needs to be assured regularly that our thought-worlds are sound and reliable. A friend can help us to see that we are wrong, or could help us to see that we are right about some part of our thinking. We may have vigorous discussions about different attitudes that we hold — but our friends are very likely to be very similar to us in many of our attitudes and interests so that these discussions are more likely to be supportive than destructive. However, we all know the anger and pain that follow a really serious disagreement with a close friend — much more unpleasnt than a disagreement with an enemy. What we should deduce from all this is that we seek out as friends those people who help to support our thought-world-personality, and we feel chastened, sapped or undermined when they do not provide it.

What sorts of people best provide the kind of personality support that I have described here as the central need of friendship and the goal that guides all effective friend-making? In the first instance, such support is provided by people who share our way of thinking. The more thought-ways we share with someone, the easier it is to communicate with that person: we can assume that our words and presumptions will be understood more easily by someone who is 'our type' than by someone who is not. We shall not have the repetitious discomfort of perpetually explaining ourselves, our meanings and our jokes.

Yet there is much more to it than this, although it has taken researchers a long time to sort out the confusing detail of the picture. For one thing, the type of similarity that we need to share with someone in order to communicate effectively depends on the stage that the relationship has reached. At early stages it is quite enough that acquaintances are broadly similar, but at later stages the similarity must be more precise, refined and detailed. One of the skills of friendmaking is to know what sorts of similarity to look for at which times as the relationship proceeds: similarity of attitudes is fine at the early to middle stages, but matters much less later if the partners do not work at discovering similarities in the ways that they view other people. Very close friends must share the same sorts of framework for understanding the actions, dispositions and characters of other people in general, and in specific instances of mutual acquaintance. Such similarity is rare and prized. For that reason, if for no other, it is painful and extremely significant to lose it.

Loss or absence of particular friends deprives us of some measure of support for our personality and it is essential to our psychological health that we have the skill to avoid this. Losing a friend not only makes us die a little, it leaves bits of our personality floating in the air, and can make people fall apart psychologically. Of course, it will depend on how much our personality has been supported by that partner, which particular parts are involved, how readily they are supported by other friends, how much time we have had to anticipate and adjust to the loss, and so on. But essentially the loss or absence of friends and close satisfying relationships does not merely cause anxiety, grief or depression; it can cause other, more severe, forms of psychological disintegration or deterioration, often with the physical and mental side-effects noted earlier. Many of the well-known psychosomatic illnesses and hysterical states are actually caused by relationship problems, although this has not been realised by as many doctors as one might expect. For too long the accepted medical folklore has assumed that the person's inner mental state is a given, and that it causes psychosomatic effects when it gets out of balance. It is now quite clear that the surest way to upset people's mental balance is to disturb their close relationships. We need friends to keep us healthy both physically and mentally: therefore it is doubly important that we perfect the ways of gaining and keeping friends. An important first step is to recognise the different needs that each relationship can fulfil for us, and the means by which this can be achieved.

In the rest of this book I will consider the normal marriage, the normal family, the normal close friendship, and the casual acquaintance as instances of relationships that need to be cherished and maintained. The nature of distressed marriages, disturbed families and so on will also be given some attention but it is not possible to do justice to those special problems fully here. Equally I have not singled out homosexual relationships for special mention since in their conduct and maintenance they are very little different from heterosexual ones: there are similar problems of meeting partners, developing the relationship, negotiating suitable behaviours and so on. There are also different problems, too, as there are with courtship as distinct from relationships at work, or nonsexual male-female adult friendships as distinct from parent-child relationships. Each kind of relationship is a little bit unique with its own special style and character. But it is also a big bit similar to other relationships. Accordingly I am focussing on the normal ones perhaps in the statistical sense of 'normal', that is, the most commonly occurring ones, the ones familiar to the greatest number of people. I shall look at how these change during a person's life cycle, how they develop, and what can go wrong. In particular I shall stress the actions and skills that need to be accomplished to cope with the beginnings and the subsequent growth of these relationships: friendship is action, friendship is skill. It involves four separate accomplishments: (i) recognising, selecting and making the most of appropriate opportunities for friendship. This involves a sliding scale of subtle judgements about people and about situations: accordingly it is the point where most people go wrong most often; (ii) having a range of strategies and techniques for encouraging and enticing likeable persons into a relationship, and making them see the potental in that relationship for the satisfaction of their needs for personality support; (iii) possessing a strategic armoury and an adequate repertoire of knowledge about the ways in which relationships are helped to develop and grow. This involves knowledge of how to pace a relationship so that it progresses at a rate that is satisfactory to both partners; (iv) having a set of skills that help to maintain and repair relationships. They need overhaul, maintenance and servicing just like any other dynamic structure does, and this is often overlooked.

All of these activities are important for proper and successful relationships, not just the first one (i.e. meeting people). Also important is the fact that relationships can be lost because the individual fails to perform any one of these four activities adequately. It is not just because a person does not meet people, or because a person is not outwardly attractive, that he or she may have no friends. Some people meet a lot of other people but simply cannot sustain attraction, or are attractive to the 'wrong' sorts of people, or — most unpleasant of all — develop relationships initially and cannot maintain them.

So there are many ideas about friendship that need fuller explanation not only from the point of view of correcting presently ill-informed or misconceived notions, but also from the wider perspective of changes in social policy. Very many people who are poor at forming relationships, or who are severely and directly affected by other people's relationship deficiencies, are obvious inhabitants of our social casualty departments, such as the divorce courts, remand homes, prisons, mental hospitals, battered women's hostels, and community homes. Other groups are also, at root, suffering from relationship difficulties. Such groups include would-be suicides, depressives, some neurotics, some alcoholics — even some violent prisoners, rapists and child-molesters (Howells, 1981). We should also think of including some people with illnesses that were once thought to be purely physical, but on closer inspection are seen to be caused by relationship problems. All of these people are, in their own way, crying for a kind of help that only a fuller understanding of friendship can provide — understanding of how friendships start, develop and are sustained.

Summary

In this chapter I have stressed the serious and far-reaching medical and psychological consequences that follow from disturbances or loss of relationships, including sleep disorders, anxiety, depression, headaches and general ill-health. I have noted the research which evaluates the reasons why we have friends, and I have indicated that the most important of these reasons is the provision of personality support — that is, the bolstering and propping up of our beliefs and opinions. Friends help to cushion our personalities and reassure us about our value as people. I have shown that the type of support and the areas of personality supported will change dramatically and extensively as relationships develop. Proper relating thus presupposes a skilful recognition of how relationships are paced and how their development is fed, and I have begun to show that we need a lot of unconscious skills to make friends properly. It is essential for satisfying relationships that the partners have the ability to provide one another with the 'right' sorts of personality support at the right time. In stressing the different stages and types of relationships I have begun to indicate that friend-making is a complex skill with many parts (starting, developing and maintaining) each of which will be explored in a subsequent chapter.

Note

1. See annual reports to SSRC, September 1980-August 1981 on the project entitled The Social Psychology of Long Term Relationships issued by Michael Argyle at Oxford University.

2

Perfect Strangers and the Action of Attraction

The previous chapter has indicated the needs that friendship satisfies, and has noted that many separable skills comprise the means of achieving friendships that are capable of satisfying these needs. In the present chapter I shall survey some of the scientific evidence that has been amassed about the starting of friendships. It will soon become apparent that many misconceptions have been exposed by such work, particularly the belief that we start friendships on the basis of personal qualities. On the contrary, it will begin to become clear that although each person does undoubtedly bring something to relationships as an individual, it is their *behaviour* that matters most at the very start, and later the attraction is cemented by joint, not individual, action. Relationships have to be created and forged jointly by trust, sharing of secrets, intimacy, confidence in another's advice, and emotional support in times of trouble. But these things must be allowed to take time to emerge in a relationship and cannot be rushed. Initially the two partners must draw themselves to one another and hint that such delightful depths may later be achieved. How is this crucial entry to friendship properly devised?

It is a mistake to assume that first impressions from outward appearance are of most importance in starting off a good friendship, and it is naïve to think that physical appearance is the vital force for attraction, or that people who look attractive just 'have it made'. Such mistaken beliefs merely invite the unwary into a social ghost-train with many nasty surprises in store, and also help to misdirect their attention away from the knowledge, judgements and actions that really matter. Relationships are based on the activities and skills of the partners. Skilful partners comprehend the 'ecology of friendship' — the places where it can be fostered, persons to whom it can be offered, the range of activities that is permitted at each stage of friendship, and so on. They also develop and employ effective skills of judgement and person perception — that is, they are attentive to the tell-tale signs by which other people give off information about their character and secret fears. They know what to communicate, when and how to do it in a way that avoids their being dismissed, disregarded or rendered 'invisible'. By focusing on these three active constituents of the chemistry of friendship, the present chapter will begin to stress the actions of attraction, and flesh out the behavioural skills involved at the very start of relationships.

Attraction — the very first point of a relationship — is important not only for people seeking to set up a long-term friendship, nor is it solely of interest to individuals who sense that they may be bad at it. Each satisfying and longlasting relationship starts at the point where two strangers meet, both for people who are quite good at getting relationships going and for those who are not. When the attraction stage goes badly the rest of the potential relationship never materialises. It is also a key point for sales personnel, doctors, bank staff, and anyone dealing with the public for short encounters whose success depends on getting things off on the right foot even for a very short time. The skills are different from the ones that come into play later when the encounter gets moving and is turned into a relationship, and I shall take a further two chapters to consider the skills involved there. At the present stage, I shall be looking at the ways of arousing friendship drives, of dealing with the fears that make people wary of entering relationships; techniques to combat the effects of prejudice and stereotyping; methods of avoiding disregard or 'invisibility'; and the research knowhow that shows how people capitalise on the attraction stage of relationships. Each of these areas yields a different sort of practical help and advice about how to put friend making together into a working whole.

Fostering Friendships: The Ecology of Place and Time

At first sight it looks as if the best advice that can be given to a lonely person is that he should try to meet as many people as possible, go forth and multiply the number of acquaintances that he encounters, and generally immerse himself in contacts with other persons. One artificial way of doing this is to sign up with a dating agency. The agency asks a number of questions and arranges a partner on the basis of the answers given by the applicant and by the partner that they choose. It is then up to the individual to meet the partner and to make it all work, and lack of ability to do this may have been the person's real problem in the first place! So the agency is no use at all for people who do not know what to do once they meet their partner, and such people are just being cruelly encouraged to pay a lot of money merely to get rejected more and more often, by more and more people. Such people need to change their friendship behaviour, and brush up their relationship knowhow first. The many artificial ways of meeting people — like parties, singles bars and dating agencies — do all offer the chance of meeting a partner who is interested in a relationship, but they do not offer any general help on how to attract other people outside of these very special circumstances. In fact, they simply stack the cards and do not guarantee anything — especially, they guarantee nothing about the activities of friendship that will ultimately be necessary.

One other subtle reason can be given why they are fallacious. Dating agencies are misleadingly comfortable for people who have difficulty deciding when to be friendly and when not to be because the situation is well-defined: both people who sign up for the adventure know they are doing it and what is expected; they know what the situation is like. The persons have to exercise no skill or judgement to recognise the situation; they simply have to try and act in a way that encourages other people to play up to the role that the situation demands of them. The situation itself contains these demands and they are known to everyone involved. Because of this the situation actually side-steps a problem: some people founder in relationships because they do not normally know what is called for, or do not recognise the demands, and the limits, of the situation. The member of a loyal crowd who offers the Queen a cigarette is such a person. The job interviewee who invites the chairman out for a drink is another. These people fail to recognise that not all friendliness should be taken as personal, nor should it be seen to invite initiation of a close relationship. On the other side of the coin, there are people who do not pay careful attention to the problem of recognising when friendly advances are called for, and need to have it all spelt out so clearly as to be embarrassing for everyone. They are perhaps too shy or wary to open up and relax; or they may simply not realise what is necessary; or, recognising it, may not have the skills to carry it out reliably.

It is perhaps surprising to realise that such a problem exists, but a whole field of research has been devoted to it (the so-called 'social skills' research that explores the minute behaviours of social interaction (Argyle, 1978; Trower, *et al.*, 1978; Trower, 1981)). An example from my personal experience of this difficulty was when I was in a hurry once, and running to an appointment. One of my pupils, an awkward girl with minor behavioural problems, rushed up to me in the drizzle and thrust into my hand a piece of birthday cake wrapped in a paper bag. Evidently she had just celebrated her 21st birthday, had a secret crush on me, and was trying to start something going. Soggy birthday cake in the drizzle when I was in a rush would seem like a pretty poor way to start, but she clearly did not realise this. Not everyone knows how to 'read' the situation and to reserve the attempt at friendmaking until a suitable moment. There is even a story of a boss who once tried to introduce one of his members of staff to a distinguished visitor when they all chanced to meet in the urinal, a place that actually makes it rather difficult to carry out normal greeting and handshaking in a satisfactory way.

The first stage of making friendships is an understanding of the ecology of attraction; that is to say, a grasp of the situations and circumstances in which attraction is 'permitted' (or even expected), and also of the places or occasions when it is not. Most people would have little difficulty recognising the fact that situations differ in their demands for sociable action, but some people need either formal intervention from clinical psychologists or counsellors, or perhaps just some firm guidance by associates who can indicate that they need to focus on such things. People who seem unfriendly at parties may not be hostile, they may just be ignorant of the ecology of friendship and the skills required to capitalise on it. Some of this involves merely the ability to recognise when it is desirable to turn on the range of friendship behaviours discussed in the next two chapters, but other components involve recognition or reading of the features of social interactions that are seemingly insignificant and yet have enormous power.

Some situations are good for friendship and some are not; some are good for some people and not others; some are good for starting friendship and some are suitable only once the relationship has its independent life. An important skill to acquire and develop, then, relies on two features of relationship ecology: first, one must recognise situations that are appropriate to the starting of a particular sort of relationship; second, one must learn to choose, emphasise and seek out those activities and situations that are appropriate to the systematic and successful development of the relationship so started. For instance, research shows that when we like people we not only feel strongly positive about them, we actually do different things with them and meet them in different places (Argyle *et al.*, 1981). We should change this pattern as we come to know them and like them better. We usually try to meet liked people more often in places where food and drink are served; disliked people are encountered in places where work is done. Liked people are met for longer periods of time and the meeting is usually less structured or focused than is a meeting with someone we dislike. In short, friendship and non-friendship are expressed not only through different feelings but through a totally different range of activities and situations. It is important to learn to recognise and distinguish them and develop the range of skills that is necessary to cope with them in a way appropriate to our wishes. Someone who wants to be friendly first has to arrange for the meeting to take place in a suitable environment, without time pressure, and where both partners can feel relaxed. Then he should ensure that the meeting is not overstructured or focused on a task. Meetings should not always be short, and eating or drinking should be encouraged during the whole business!

Different kinds of relationships happen in different sorts of environment and also involve different activities. Work relationships are work relationships rather than friendships, not simply because of how the people feel about one another, but because of where they happen and what the people do together. (Mangham, 1981). People define and accept the relationship because of what they do together as much as vice versa. Indeed, studies have shown that it is possible to alter someone's feelings about another person merely by getting them to do different activities together, or to meet in different places. Thus, factory workmates who are given the job of organising a factory allotment or a Christmas party, or who are asked to meet outside the factory in a pub or café to discuss such informal matters will respond to the cues in the situation. Here they are doing friendly things in a friendly environment — therefore they must be friends! This involves so-called 'self-perception', that is, where people catch themselves doing something and explain it *afterwards* in a way that makes sense. When workmates meet in a friendly situation, are not focused on their usual work routine, do the activities that friends normally do, and enjoy themselves, then they explain all that as being due to their friendship or liking for one another, rather than as due to the fact that they were asked to meet there. Such a result seemed to follow from the careful arrangement of the Camp David talks where, on expert advice, the US President placed President Sadat and Prime Minister Begin — two political opponents — in a situation where they were focused on daily human routine, rather than on political routine. By all accounts they slept in rooms near one another, ate together, saw what each other looked like in the morning, and generally came to see the human side of each other rather than the distant, political, stereotyped side. They got on better in their talks and came to trust one another more.

The differences between work and play seem to the unskilled eye to matter very little. In fact they are, on the contrary, extremely significant in relationships, not because of what they are but because of how they make people see one another. The activities that we perform in the company of another person are crucial ways of defining the relationship to that person, and if we seek to become friends with someone it is essential to enter

37

situations, and create opportunities, where activities that 'feel friendly' can be done. And as I shall show in the following two chapters, such activities *must* alter if the relationship is to grow and develop.

Aside from general differences between situations like this, there are some differences between men and women in respect of friendship — just as there are between older and younger people. For instance, men fall in love sooner than women, but women fall out of love sooner than men. In a long-term study of courtship (Hatfield and Traupmann, 1981) it was found that women operate a last-in-first-out principle in this sort of relationship, whereas men are first-in-last-out. When one also hears of the studies of marital satisfaction showing that men appear to be generally happier and more content with their marriages than their wives are, then it appears that some general difference between the sexes has been discovered. However, it depends very much on the sort of relationship contemplated, and we have found in the Lancaster research programme that men are generally much worse at starting friendships when they can be overheard or closely observed, whereas women can do it as successfully under these conditions as under any other (Miell and Duck, 1982). Obviously, someone attempting to start a friendship with a man would be better doing it in either a private, quiet place where they cannot be overheard, or else in a noisy public place where they do not feel the particular focus of attention.

However, a very important aspect of friendmaking is the fact that there are significant changes in activities as the relationship grows. Just as we behave differently towards people whom we like and dislike, meeting in different situations and performing different types of activity, so we distinguish close and casual acquaintances in the same way. For example, in one of my own studies it was found that people who are becoming friends tend to meet one another in public places more often than in private for as long as six weeks into the relationship, and then they meet in private more often. When the relationship is just starting, people tend to feel that the other person initiates activities more than they do — and this is important because it gives a strong sense of the other person's desire to foster the relationship, and makes people feel needed and wanted. It is evidently important to stress, when initiating encounters in this way, that they are being suggested because the other person's company, rather than the task or pastime itself, is the desired 'target'. As things develop, however, it is equally important to ensure that no one person does all the initiating of meetings, and great care should be taken to create mutual or shared suggestions for activity, or even to stress that one's partner is doing much of this relationship work.

I have indicated some patterns of activity that differentiate friends from non-friends and I have shown that ecology matters in attraction. There are other differences that matter too, particularly those between different sorts of relationships. As may be judged from the above, people starting friendships with colleagues at work need to create different sorts of situations and meetings from those wishing to enter a courtship, and the research indicates a need to focus on different features of the partner also. Meetings with colleagues will usually focus on the task or work involved, but can be transformed and personalised by attention to the so-called socio-emotional content of the interaction: work can be dealt with briskly in a task-oriented way, or it can be handled in a more leisurely, person-oriented way. Comments about the way in which the other person is coping with the task, about the atmosphere in the meeting, about one's enjoyment of the encounter, and so on, are all contributors to a raised socio-emotional level, and can personalise the meeting in a way that emphasises the relationship between the participants rather than the tasks that they have to complete. In the case of dating or courtship, the important activities in the first encounter are the creation of mutual interest in the partners, an indication of concern over the partner's welfare, and the instigation of a wish for future meetings where the partner's values, opinions and attitudes can be explored. I shall say more about this in the next chapter since it is one of the most significant skills in developing relationships in general.

The Skills of Judging Relationship Needs

A variation on such necessary skills is the ability to recognise when, even in the right circumstances, the other person is resistant to entering a relationship. Sometimes this is a matter of understanding what their posture, facial expression or vocal tone actually means; sometimes it requires a deeper appreciation of their character or their self-image and their beliefs about their own worth. In some cases the two go very closely together: people who think very little of themselves give it away by their bodily movements, facial expressions or their tone of voice. For instance, their posture may be dejected, their eye movements may be nervous, and their tone of voice flat. They mumble rather than speaking out clearly and confidently; they avoid looking at the person they are talking to; they lick their lips, hold their hands in front of their mouths when talking, and move in an agitated way. Many of these signs are similar to those looked for by police officers and customs officers: it is as if persons with low self-esteem are feeling *permanently* guilty — guilty for being themselves. It is important to spend some time looking at this because much of what I shall say runs counter to the usual hidden assumption in our particular culture that everyone wants friends, wants them to an equal degree at all times or in all situations, and wants to expand their network of friends whenever possible. On the contrary, extensive research shows that there are some blatant and many subtle errors in this belief.

For one thing, it has been shown reliably that different people have different levels of drive for friendship, not only from time to time, but also as permanent features of their personality (Schachter, 1959; Duck, 1977). It is as normal to enjoy a close, small, intense set of friendships as it is to prefer to have lots of friends. It is even perfectly normal, but not very common, for someone to desire no friends at all. As demonstrated in chapter 1, a fundamental purpose of friendship is the provision of reassurance that other people need and want us, but a few self-assured individuals are strong enough to carry on alone. Some are absorbed in work that takes them away from sociable activities, or have such close ties with their family that they do not need to step outside to find further reassurance of their worth. Along similar lines, some people have very low sex drives and, unless they feel uncomfortable about it, there is not really anything wrong with that. Equally, not every isolated person is unhappy about being isolated, although most are. What is important in friendmaking is recognising and coping with these differences, particularly when encountering strangers whose drive for new friendships may be at a very different level from one's own. One way to help in this is to try and understand where such differences come from so that we can be most efficient in dealing with them when we encounter them.

Friendship drives are affected by two things: first, the person's global and relatively stable beliefs about his general worth and value as a person; second, temporary or transient features of people's lives and circumstances. The former influence can be made up of self-esteem, experiences in prior relationships, beliefs about personal physical or social attractiveness, and general expectations about what rewards can be obtained in relationships. The temporary, transient set of influences comprise recent experiences, whether they have just broken off or just started a deep relationship, whether they have just had fortuitous experiences that make them feel good, and so on. Whilst these latter ones are worth considering in more detail later in the chapter, it is obviously the first, more permanent features that need closest attention.

People who have frequently experienced rejection in the past, and who blame themselves for it, are likely to maintain low drives towards friendship through fears of further humiliation (Mehrabian and Ksionzky, 1974). They will be likely to remain socially unadventurous, reserved and cautious, will feel vulnerable in new relationships, will need to be frequently reminded that the partner likes them, and may be vigilant and suspicious. They often express the deepest cynicism and doubts about other people's motives in relating to them, and are constantly on the watch for signs that the other person is insincere, or is entering a relationship with them for instrumental reasons, like a desire for sex. Although such fears and doubts are most often shaped by experiences as a young adult, adolescent or child (which is one reason why we should attend more closely to relationship development in children, see chapter 5) they can be sustained by what happens in adulthood — and likewise can be broken by the same means as a very famous experiment shows. This particular study was based on the controversial view that our personality and our usual mode of behaviour are based on the way other people treat us, rather than on something in ourselves.

In a study before the Second World War, of a kind perhaps not ethically acceptable today (Guthrie, 1938), a class of male students was invited to pay attention to a rather unattractive girl (unbeknownst to her) and to treat her as if she were very attractive. They began to compliment her on the way she looked and moved, began to ask her for dates and started to respond to her as if she were highly attractive. At first there was little noticeable effect, but gradually she started to take more care over her appearance, to buy more fashionable clothes, and even to act in a more attractive manner. After a while, the boys really were not pretending when they complimented her: she really had become a very attractive young woman and was sought after by other boys on the campus, not just ones privy to the experiment. Her view of herself had been fundamentally restructured by the responses that she received from other people and she acted in accord with the new view.

Over time such experiences lead people to think in a very rigid way about their social encounters. In another experiment on people with both high and low self-esteem (i.e. some people who felt that they were valuable people, and others who felt worthless) the far-reaching effects of this were strikingly demonstrated (Stroebe, 1977). The group heard someone say something about them which was either complimentary or critical, and their task was to guess whether the person was giving their true opinion, or was acting under instructions from the experimenter. Subjects with high self-esteem usually guessed that a compliment was 'true opinion', whilst a criticism was 'instructions'. Subjects with low self-esteem habitually believed the reverse: criticisms were true opinion, and praise must have been instructed by the experimenter. In real life this effect would have hidden but far-reaching consequences. For instance, if you are talking to someone at a party who goes off to get another drink you may treat this differently as a result of how you feel about yourself. A person with high self-esteem will assume that the partner was thirsty; a person with low-esteem may assume that the partner was bored by the conversation. To be sure that someone with low self-esteem is not provided with further 'evidence about their unworthiness', it is always worth making it clear that circumstances, rather than they themselves, are what has led one to leave them in such a situation!

Recognising that these differences exist and can affect not only an individual's behaviour but also the whole way that he approaches and interprets other people's social actions, we need to sensitise ourselves to their significance. A person who has low self-esteem should practise considering alternative explanations for other people's social actions, particularly focusing on alternatives that do not involve self-flagellation. The very fact of being able to create a long list of alternative explanations may help such a person acquire a sense of proportion that focuses less on self-perceived unworthiness, and more on the realities of social life as enjoyed by others. On the other hand, a person who suspects that his partner is someone afflicted with the vigilance bred of low-esteem needs to adopt a strategic style in behaviour that reassures the partner and lays any wariness to rest. One needs to spend much less time talking about oneself and more time inviting the other person to present himself, steering away from disagreement or dogmatic statements, and towards an attentive and accepting, if gently interpretative, manner. One can adopt deliberate summarising of what the person says ('I see. So you think that...'), attentive reference to past points ('You said a moment ago that...'), and invitations to expand their views in an unthreatening way ('That's interesting. I'd like you to tell me more about that.'). These all stress one's interest and so can lay the ghost of the person's vigilance. It is a simple style and strategy that emphasise one's regard for them as people. Stress on their own successful action is also important. As a very subtle example, I know a man who never says 'Congratulations' to someone who has had a success; he always says 'Well done', thus stressing not the good fortune itself but the individual's own contribution to bringing it about!

Low self-esteem is not the only influence that makes people wary of embarking on relationships; there are complex processes that prevent people carrying out their desires for relationships. For instance, it is commonly believed that physically attractive people have better relationships and more opportunities, but this common belief has been shown to be false. Men may desire attractive-looking women more often than unattractive ones, but are more nervous of approaching them and experience high fears of rejection. In fact, then, people have a series of psychological 'governors' that stop them approaching all the partners who are apparently the choicest from a purely physical point of view (Berscheid and Walster, 1974). In this case the men do not invariably ask out the most attractive women: they seek out those who are as attractive as they think they can allure without fear of rejection. The 'governor' here is the man's level of self-esteem and confidence.

There are two forms of such self-esteem that have been explored by research: a global and relatively permanent form, and a temporary or vicarious form. The global form has been referred to as *level of aspiration* and, briefly, it describes the level at which the person sets his sights: it defines the level of attractiveness of the kind of partner that the person is confident that they can draw (Murstein, 1977; Stroebe, 1977). Research indicates that people with similar levels of aspiration tend to marry one another. Their 'objective' physical attractiveness may be very different from their level of aspiration: some very beautiful people do not think they are very attractive, and some unattractive people are confident that their sparkling wit compensates and makes them more valuable socially.

In the case of the temporary or vicarious level of self-esteem there have been many experiments where men have been given false results on an intelligence test (in order to make them feel either very good or very bad about themselves) and then tested with a female accomplice of the experimenter. The accomplice is made up in a way that makes her look attractive or unattractive, and the idea is to see whether the man tries to arrange a date with her. Sure enough, men who have their esteem vicariously raised by being told that they have scored very highly on the test are much more likely to chat up the confederate when she is attractive!

The effects of self-esteem are often general and affect all of someone's behaviour, not just actions in a beginning relationship. However, researchers have also discovered other psychological 'governors' that affect people's willingness to become involved in relationships. Individuals have other general friendship drives that affect their vigilance and their trust of other people; and they also have some very specific beliefs about the level of satisfaction that they can expect in different sorts of relationships. Researchers (e.g. Thibaut and Kelley, 1959; Miller and Parks, 1982) talk of an individual's *comparison level*, that is, the general level of satisfaction or 'profit' that an individual has come to expect from relationships during the course of his or her life. If the individual suspects that a new relationship will bring rewards in excess of the comparison level then he will be attracted to it: otherwise not. However, sometimes people enter and stay in relationships that are below this comparison level simply because they know that they could not, at present, do any better. In short, they also have a *comparison level for alternatives* — a belief about the level of satisfaction or profit that they could obtain in alternative relationships of a similar type (e.g. with alternative dates or friends). Comparison level and comparison level for alternatives may be different because the former refers to all relationships in general, and the latter refers only to specific sorts of relationships at a particular time. People in a relationships that lies above their comparison level for alternatives (that is, people who do not think that they could 'do better' in another relationship) are obviously dependent on that relationship, even if they are not happy with it. A knowledge of what people feel about their relationships and their views of alternatives can help an outsider to decide the level of the friendship drive and to direct effort accordingly.

Such things as self-esteem, level of aspiration, drives for friendship and comparison levels are relatively permanent or enduring aspects of an individual's style. There are also some temporary features that affect behaviour in relationships. For one thing, friendship needs are known to be influenced by a kind of critical mass phenomenon: once a person's friendships reach a certain number the person seems to lose the desire to seek out any more friends, and usually does not do so except at the expense of existing friends (Duck, 1977). Furthermore, there appears to be a critical threshold before a person feels motivated to do anything about isolation or loneliness (Perlman and Peplau, 1981): it takes time to attack the roots of the person's psychology enough for him to take action. He must perceive a large discrepancy between what he achieves in relationships and what he desires. Not only this, but commitment to the relationship must have reached a low point since, for some types of relationship like marriage and relationships at work, one's personal commitment may be lower than the formal, structural commitment (that is, one's liking for the relationship may not match up to the social pressures that keep one in it, such as pressures from relatives or friends, legal obligations or contractual partnerships (Johnson, 1982)).

It is also usual to think of the arrival of a competitor as the cause of a relationship's ending: when a rival turns up, the partner runs off with the rival. A moment's thought enables us to share with recent research the view that this is wrong. What matters is not that a rival just turns up, but the fact that the partner *accepts* the rival. In other words, the important feature of the situation is the psychological state of the person who desires the rival. Clearly, willingness to become involved with a new partner at the expense of an old-established one is the key change that has taken place. Personal commitment has reached a point at which structural commitment can be ignored: the repulsion from the relationship reaches a negative force that is powerful enough to ovecome the social compulsions that bind one to it. At such points of climactic decision, the person decides to ignore the structural commitments through lack of personal commitment: the decision to run off with the neighbour's wife depends not only on the neighbour's wife, but on one's own views of the alternative. Thus a person's friendship drives affect actions more strongly than do external forces and constraints.

A final influence on these friendship drives is presented by a combination of age and place in the life-cycle (Dickens and Perlman, 1981). At certain ages a person is more likely to be searching for particular sorts of relationships and is more likely to be active in attempts to expand his social network. Thus mid-adolescence is the time where a demand to enter heterosexual relationships becomes dominant, and a strong pressure to seek a marriage partner is exerted on people of the age group between sixteen and thirty. We can expect such individuals to be on the look out for sexual, cohabital or marital partners rather more noticeably than very much older or very much younger people would be. Also it is found that friendship drives decline sharply after the age of thirty or so, except for people who experience serious disruptions in their life, such as divorce, change of career, or death of spouse. For such disrupted people there is actually a very sudden and marked increase in social involvements — a fact not without its own psychological problems and stresses since it runs counter to the social pattern that they would normally have expected. The usual lull lasts until just before retirement age when a vigorous spurt in social activity precedes a gradual but steady decline in the number of friends (usually through their death rather than from an increase in quarrelling).

The significance of all the foregoing influences on friendship drives lies in their importance not only to people who wish to improve their friendships, but also to those who wish to help and counsel those who have that wish. Friendships, courtships and even casual relationships are begun only when the partners wish to enter them. By attending to the life-cycle position, social circumstances and personality style of the individual one can more easily gauge their likely interest in a relationship. Access to a relationship follows only when we correctly exercise a skilled judgement that the circumstances and the person would both be right for us to make the effort. If the need for the relationship is not present, or cannot be skilfully stimulated then all the correct friendly behaviour in the world will be to no avail.

The right sorts of acquired knowledge about relationship ecology and influences on friendship drives constitute the first skill that must be acquired for successful relating, then. It is possible for individuals to be formally schooled in such matters and for this information to be acquired where it is otherwise deficient (Trower *et al.*, 1978). Such programmes of training involve instruction on the recognition of different sorts of situations, the actions that are appropriate in them (see below (pp. 53-8 for more details), and an increased sensitivity to other people's likely friendship needs and desires. In part, this sensitivity is achieved by guided rediscovery of the means by which people indicate their interest in relationships and their availability to enter them; but in part it is achieved merely by indicating to the individual that such things need close attention and are worthy of heedful regard. In the latter case such programmes really emphasise that the skills can be practised personally, partly as suggested earlier merely by thinking about and recollecting encounters that one has observed; and partly by observing places where strangers are 'inducted' into existing groups (e.g. at parties, in clubs, at meetings, in colleges, dating agencies and singles bars). On such occasions a great deal can be learnt from the patterns in the greeting and friendly behaviour that people there exhibit. This takes us on to the next set of skills.

The next set of skills rely on different types of judgement. They depend not so much on the ability to recognise situations that are ripe with relationship promise, nor on the skill of recognising when someone's friendship drive is correctly aroused. Rather they depend on the ability to recognise an individual who has a high statistical likelihood of being a suitable companion. The research shows very clearly that people are uninventive in their choice of partners, and that those who attempt to form relationships outside of usual boundaries are probably wasing their time (Kerckhoff, 1974; Rodin, 1982). People making friends actually direct their efforts discriminately as is clear from the following research findings. Friendships are usually formed with people of the same religion and socio-economic level, who have a similar job, similar background, similar educational history, similar level of income, similar recreational interests, and similar racial origins. Naturally the research that finds this is generalised, and exceptions are frequent. However, as a productive strategy for increasing the likelihood of relational success, it makes perfect sense for a person to direct attention to the group of eligible people rather than to ineligible ones. That is to say, it makes sense to recognise and to focus on people who are broadly similar to oneself as the most likely way to find personality support — again recognising that I am dealing here with the strategy that is suitable for the initiation of relationship rather than for later points.

It takes little skill and judgement to recognise people from one's own racial background, and most people would not want to exclude the possibility of cross-racial friendships anyway. However, it seems more of a task to discover similarity of religion, recreational interests, background and educational history. In fact it is easier than it seems at first sight because people are likely to try to reveal such information quite early on in an encounter. For one obvious case, people of similar recreational interests tend to congregate at the same recreational facilities: people you meet on the squash courts probably share your liking for squash, and this can be deduced merely from the ecology of the encounter, merely from where it takes place. For another thing, people usually present themselves in a way that gives the practised observer clues about them. The first couple of minutes of conversation with someone are points where they attempt to get across to others the central features of their 'person' as they see it. Although the research has only just begun to explore the ways in which people do this — for they can be extremely complicated and sophisticated — it does indicate the absolute significance of those first few vital minutes. The obvious way of doing it is to rely on social introductions. When a person is introduced to someone else by a mutual friend their name is usually given along with a brief description or 'package' that helps them to be 'located'. Research at Oxford (Collett, 1982) has shown that these packages usually consist of an indication of the introducer's relationship to the person introduced ('my mother', 'my girlfriend', 'my boss') or else that they describe what the person does ('the local teacher', 'our area sales representative', 'the golf club president'). Both types of package serve to locate the person who is introduced: they help other people to sum up their social characteristics, and to work out what kind of things to say next in order to find out more about them. Introductions like this thus help to cut down some of the judgemental work that we otherwise have to do: it might take a long time for us to work out just from looking at them that someone was the local teacher — with the educational background, income level, and so on that that implies. So an introduction from a mutal friend cuts down that work. It also effectively tells both persons introduced that they may be suitable for a relationship: if both people are already in the social networks of their mutual friend then they must start out fairly similar in all the ways that raise the probability of a successful start to a relationship.

Of course we do not always have the benefit of introductions, but an attentive listener can still pick up much useful information from the first few minutes. Many people start sentences with phrases like 'Well, I was adopted, and I think that . . .', or 'I live in Surbiton and I've noticed that . . .', or 'When I was in America on a scholarship, I found that . . .'. These are all ways of presenting to other people some marker that helps to locate the speaker and defines some feature of themselves that they regard as crucial or overbrimmingly important. It is fundamental to starting off relationships that one listens for such things and

49

attends to them. People very often introduce into their conversations phrases or ideas that are strictly redundant and illogical, but which serve a vital social and relational purpose by telling the listener things about themselves that they want to have known. It can be as simple as the phrases 'Those of us with Italian connections...', or 'My Jewish mother always used to say...', and so on. A person who slips in such information clearly wants it to be known, and wants the listener to pick it up. It is important to them, and it tells something about their way of life, their inner self and their system of values. The clearest example I ever experienced was from a girl who spoke to me when I was talking about different cultures and said, 'I was very interested in what you just said because my father died when I was eight and my mother and I lived in America.' The sentence *appears* to be concerned with the topic but its actual purpose is to tell me that she has had a difficult life with several unusual experiences: the part about the death of her father is logically irrelevant to the rest of the sentence, but socially very significant to the understanding of what she thinks is important about herself.

There are endless examples of such attempts to locate oneself, to leak information that one thinks is significant, and to get across quickly some feature or characteristic of oneself that one is just dying for the other person to know about. Indeed, the Greeks had a whole myth about these almost uncontrollable ways to leak information. Midas's barber was the only person who knew that the king had donkey's ears underneath his turban and was so overwhelmed with the knowledge that he dug a hole and whispered the secret into it. But it looks as if there is something of Midas's barber in all of us. What matters for relationships is to watch out for, attend to, and use the information that people do try to give out in this way. If it matters to them, it matters to relationships with them.

The relational reason why they do it is to individuate themselves, to make themselves 'visible', and to distinguish themselves from the mass of other people that are available for appreciation. In this way they are actually helping the rest of us if only we listen to them. For in cases where we are not given such individual information, we truly have very little to go on when we meet someone for the first time and are more or less bound to rely on stereotypes. What these individuators are doing is trying to undercut the stereotypes that may otherwise be used, because of the normal difficulties of finding out about people in a short space of time without such help.

Given that the aim of relationships is to obtain some support for our personality we need to make quick judgements about the people that we meet, and to form quick assessments of how far we would expect that a person like that could offer us the support that we need. How is this done? In most cases we all rely on stereotypes, both general and personal. Whole libraries of research papers testify to the existence of cultural stereotypes that describe particular nationalities, groups and subgroups. However, each person also has his own personal stack of such stereotypes and the true task that each of us faces is in practising their use so that we make them as accurate as possible, and as far from misleading as we can. Unfortunately, most people are influenced by outward appearance very strongly in such cases, and the only way to combat it effectively is to increase our awareness of the pitfalls. We all draw inferences about someone's personality from the way that they look, and too often these judgements are sweeping, general and unhelpful. For example, a large amount of research has shown that ugly and deformed people are assumed to be more criminally inclined than are normal-looking people (Bull, 1981): in short, we assume inward deviance from an outwardly deviant appearance. The same research shows that people with scars on their cheeks are assumed to be criminals — particularly they are assumed to be violent criminals. When asked to guess whether a scar-faced man is a lifeboatman or a prison inmate, most people assume that he is a criminal rather than someone who puts his own life at risk for others.

Other research shows that attractive-looking children are judged — even by experienced teachers and other children — to be less naughty and mischievous than are plain or ugly ones (Dion and Berscheid, 1974). When asked to judge a story of a misdeed done by a child whose photograph is attached to the story, people consistently credit the nice-looking child with nicer motivation or better reasons for doing the misdeed. Also they are less likely to claim that the act represents the child's true personality: people seem to believe that attractive-looking children are not really naughty. On the other hand, they do think that ugly children are — and they recommend tougher punishments for them. The same error occurs in court cases (Sigall and Ostrove, 1975). In one study, attractive-looking defendants were rated as less likely to be guilty than were unattractive ones, and several studies have shown that in experiments, mock jurors recommend shorter sentences for attractive people unless they used their good looks in the crime involved (e.g. if they were confidence tricksters who used their looks to distract people or lull them into unwariness).

Most of these studies use first appearance or just show photographs to people, and there is evidence that some of the effects are less powerful in real life or during extended face-to-face encounters. Even though physical appearance sets off stereotypes in all of us, we overcome them during later encounters. The real skill comes in reining in our stereotyped responses at the start and learning to control their worst effects. By learning more about how they operate, researchers have helped to show these worst effects in the clearest light. One way of overcoming them is to train oneself to think of alternative 'personalities' for strangers that one meets, to work out what different sorts of personal characteristics they may have, and to explore particularly the ways in which the stereotype does not fit. This kind of mental rehearsal helps to combat the findings about the workings of ordinary people's stereotypes, which are dreadfully consistent. Physically attractive people are judged from first appearance to have more interesting personalities, more successful careers, greater capabilities and promotion prospects — and a whole host of other perks. Evidently we do not like physically attractive people simply because they look nice — indeed this can actually scare people off as we have seen. No, the point is that ordinary people draw flattering conclusions about personalities from the way that other persons look. It is these stereotyped inferences, not the good looks alone, that are important: in short, the research tells us not *that* good looks are attractive but *why* they are responded to in the way that they are.

The important question that then follows is whether physical attactiveness favourably affects the amount of friendship or social participation that people experience. Most of us would guess the answer to be yes, and we would be right up to a point, but probably we would be wrong in detail. Researchers in the USA (Reis *et al.*, 1980) have only recently found that physically attractive people do spend their time in different ways from the rest of us. Attractive males have very many more interactions with females than they do with males — but the opposite is not true for attractive females. Evidently, attractive girls do not spend more time enjoying relationships with men than they do with other women. However, physically attractive persons of each sex reported having more fun in all their activities than the unattractive people did, even though the attractive males seemed to spend more than average amounts of time having conversations rather than actively participating in sports, or going to parties. Finally, attractive males are less likely to start off an encounter or take the social initiative, contrary to commonly held beliefs. They report that their activities are usually started jointly — when they and their partner just feel like doing something together. So although attractiveness does seem to influence our social participation, it does so more for males than for females — and not in the ways we often expect.

Whilst physical appearance affects opportunities for meeting people it does not help to make friends; it is just another circumstantial factor that affects opportunity rather than doing the creation of relationships for people, just like the other factors given so far in the chapter. Effort put in to changing one's appearance alone is largely wasted, and it would be better directed to the task of making best effective use of the opportunities for relationships that appearance may provide. The knowledge and skills outlined in the chapter so far are a good starting point, but crucial aspects of communication represent the next most important step — and I am still dealing with the very beginning of a relationship, not the ways in which it develops yet.

Communication and the Beginning of Relationships

The research in the following pages is essentially research on how people communicate information about themselves and their attitudes — their attitudes about themselves and about other people. They do this in two ways which often overlap: one concerns their so-called 'non-verbal behaviour'; the other, 'self-presentation'. The former concerns very, very subtle and slight actions, sometimes ones which are so swift that they are hard to detect unless you are looking out for them — like eye movements, changes of posture, or variations in voice pitch. Yet the information that they transmit or 'leak' is so important that it is quite enough to stop a friendship before it starts, and it is vital that people train themselves to pay attention to their style of behaviour.

This style is made up of many microscopic activities, so small that they appear superficially to be meaningless or insignificant. We do not realise the importance of such things as eye movements, however, until we focus on it. If you doubt this then try the experiment of talking to people whilst looking steadily past their right ear: do not at any time look them in the face. When the bruises have healed, pick up this book again for more information about the system of so called 'non-verbal communication' that eye movements represent.

Our eyes convey significant information about our interest in someone else: when we like someone our pupils dilate when we see them, and stay dilated whilst we talk to them (Argyle, 1969). We are not normally aware of this happening to our own eyes but we notice it when it happens to other people talking to us. Even photographs of people with dilated pupils are preferred to photographs of people with undilated pupils. Up to the middle ages women would use an infusion of deadly nightshade to dilate their pupils as a beauty aid — indeed the Latin name for deadly nightshade — *Belladonna* — means beautiful woman! Chinese jade merchants used to watch a buyer's eyes: when the pupils dilated the merchant knew that the buyer had seen a piece that he especially liked — and a skilled dealer would spot this and bargain harder about its price. The same information — dilated pupils — is used by card players as a sign that an opponent has a good hand. As our interest in someone increases, so our eyes are likely to 'leak' that information to that person — who is likely to notice, even if we do not know that the hint has been given. More importantly for active friendship, it is necessary for individuals to ensure that they pay careful attention to their partner's eyes in order to pick up any information that is given away about the partner's level of interest in starting a relationship.

The eyes give away other information that doubles their importance as an object of attention at the stages of initial attraction and beyond. Humans look at a person more often when they like him or her and they look for longer periods of time (Argyle, 1969). An intense stare can be an indication of intense liking, and a long intimate look at a person can be very rewarding and pleasant for them. When we want to look interested in someone or in what he is saying it is essential that we look closely, particularly at the eyes.

By reverse logic, when we look hard at someone he is likely to deduce that we like him, and if we avoid looking at him or look at him only for short periods, then he is likely to assume that we do not like him. Eye movements are a crucial factor in the smooth development of a relationship just as they are critical to the establishment of initial interest in starting a relationship. Talking intimately to someone whilst we look elsewhere will be less attractive than intimate conversation accompanied by correct eye movements. Talking about intimate topics is not enough: it must be stage-managed correctly.

There are many other minute behaviours that make up the full non-verbal communication system, and all of them can be used to good effect in relationship beginnings once their impact is understood (Argyle, 1969). Some are simple movements like nods that encourage people, some are to do with postures and gestures that convey one's attitudes about oneself or one's possessions. As a simple example, we all recognise that someone who puts his feet on the coffee table or desk is claiming 'ownership' of it, and simultaneously claiming to be of higher status than the person in whose presence it is done. Two people who put their feet on the same table are indicating that they are equals and that they have a relaxed relationship to one another. Such items as coffee tables, desks, furniture and clothes can be used in this way as props to convey messages about one's social status, or to ensure that one is not overlooked: we can claim space in a library or cafeteria by draping it with our props (e.g. leaving a coat over the back of a chair is a socially agreed way of reserving it, and people understand that they must ask you first before they sit in that particular chair).

However the most important ways of presenting oneself from the present point of view concern the behaviours and actions that might encourage other people to contemplate entering a relationship. Their importance stems entirely from the fact that everyone draws extensive conclusions about other people solely from what we can observe outwardly — the point that I was stressing earlier. The outward signs here concern posture, gesture and facial expression. Many scientific studies have been devoted to this area of research (Argyle, 1969). In summary it is clear that if someone adopts a relaxed posture then we shall conclude that they like us and do not find us threatening. Again, if someone smiles or nods as we talk, we shall conclude that this is an encouragement for us to carry on talking — or whatever else we were doing. The rewarding force of nods and smiles is so great that people can be encouraged by them to use more plural nouns, or more adjectives, to make more personal statements or give more opinions, or to make more sweeping gestures. (There is even a famous story about a teacher whose class conspired to nod and smile whenever he walked to the left: eventually he fell off the platform!).

Such powerful rewards are contained in these simple actions that it is important to use them effectively and focus attention carefully upon the ways that they are used. Not only do they act to invite people into relationships, they also are of great value, when properly employed, in getting people to open out and respond to overtures. People who use the non-verbal communication system inadequately will very rapidly put people off (perhaps without ever knowing why) unless someone focuses their attention gently upon their deficiency (Trower, 1981). Clinics and psychological training schools now exist to inculcate the skills in really bad cases, but for most people it is adequate merely to focus them on their use of gesture, their eye movements, and their facial expression. Air hostesses are trained to smile when talking to people; clinical patients can be trained to look at people when they talk to them; anyone can be encouraged to use such behaviours satisfactorily, as the cited reading for this chapter details. The important point is that such apparently microscopic activities have major effects on attraction.

Such a system can also be built on by a skilful style of questioning. One good place to watch this style in action is in television interviewers who are often meeting nervous strangers and having to 'open them out'. Good interviewers are able to encourage even the most taciturn interviewee to speak out. They do this partly by adopting an encouraging posture, an inviting expression and a generally relaxed and interested manner. Also they pay attention to their own style of speech and they ask questions that cannot be answered with a mere 'yes' or 'no', as so-called 'closed questions' do. On the contrary, such questions as 'How do you feel about . . . ?' or 'Can you tell us what it was like to . . . ?' are good, open-ended questions that will open people out. Lawyers tend to prefer closed questions because that gives them more control over the answers, help them to predict and direct the encounter, and appear to produce 'facts' rather than opinions. It is a very subtle stylistic difference, but researchers have shown, for instance, that jurors react differently to witnesses' answers to questions like 'Did you feel excited?' (where the answer should be just 'Yes' or 'No'), as opposed to the answer to 'How did you feel?' It seems on commonsense grounds to be quite unimportant how we phrase requests like this, but research demonstrates that, in certain circumstances, someone who says 'Can you help me? I have sprained my ankle', will get more offers of help than someone who says, 'I have sprained my ankle and I need help.' In friendship formation people who adopt closed question styles will appear over-inquisitive, nosey, overbearing and badgering, even though they may in fact be genuinely concerned and interested. On the other hand, someone who uses open-ended questions will be seen as concerned and genuinely interested in the respondent's opinions, advice and judgement.

It is therefore important that people attend to their styles in this particular way and ask questions in a manner that encourages without compelling. The differences in style are minute but important, and they depend on the non-verbal and communicational skills above for two reasons: wrong use of the skills conveys the wrong messages about a person's friendliness; inadequacy in using the skills disrupts the flow of conversation and makes it hard for people to interact (see next two chapters). What is significant, however, is that people who lack these so-called 'social skills' can be trained to improve them, with consequent good efects on their social relationships (Trower, *et al.*, 1978, Trower, 1981). I shall say more about this, particularly in the later chapter on the training of children who show social skill problems. The whole theme, however, emphasises the importance, in the early stages of friendship, of very small components of behaviour. These unacknowledged aspects of starting friendships have an important part to play in the success or failure of the resultant relationship. If we do not behave adequately in the ways described people will soon decide they do not want to explore further — and so the relationship will die at its first breath. The things we do are much more important than attractive personal characteristics or attributes. Friendships start well when they are well done — at a very basic level. What matters then is making them develop, and that requires different sorts of action and different sorts of skill.

Summary

In this chapter I have focused on the groundwork of relationships, and I have attended particularly to the way in which they start or are fostered — the skills and behaviours that get relationships going. I have stressed that it is the behaviour of attraction that matters more than other features such as good looks, and I indicated the importance of the situation in all of this. It is important first to recognise and distinguish situations that are suitable for friendship to be begun; next it is necessary to recognise partners' likely level of friendship drive, as results from their level of self-esteem, their level of aspiration, their comparison level and their general view of themself. Also important is the strategy of focusing on persons who belong to a suitable 'target' group, to whom one is initially similar in general background — people from the same social, religious, and economic group as ourselves. The ability to recognise such persons is an important skill, and so is the ability to work out or deduce their likely ability to provide personality support for oneself. Final skills at this initial stage stem from one's ability to present oneself in a friendly and inviting manner, and also to read the other person's wishes and desires from the minute, non-verbal ways in which they communicate these feelings. The skills of developing, changing and maintaining relationships build on these basic foundations.

3

Initial Developments

The moments after an initial move in attraction are busy ones. Once the partners accept that they are both interested in developing a relationship, much intelligence work has to be done, many activities have to be co-ordinated, much sharing of viewpoints is necessary. Over and above this, a major task of developing a friendship is to translate it from the private shared feelings of two individuals into a fully accepted, working, active relationship. That is, the association moves from the private to the public domain, and the partners have to let other people know that they are now partners, friends, mates or companions. To achieve this public acknowledgement of the relationship, the partners have to carry out various skilled behaviours that they have not needed before. To continue with the car driving analogy that I have already used earlier, the partners have to become less concerned with looking at the pedals, their feet, the steering wheel and the gear levers: they must being to look down the road, steer a sensible course, and make their activity fit neatly into the available pathways and patterns familiar to other road users.

This is a crucial stage in friendships: the point where they turn from mere attraction into full relationships is the point where they become most full of promises and rich in personal fulfilment. The developmental period is, however, also fraught with difficulty and risk. The intentions or desires for a relationship still need effective execution, and the developing relationship has to be put together into a working model, stage-managed, and encouraged to burgeon. Essentially, the development of relationships has two stages, each given one of these next

59

two chapters: in the present chapter I shall look at the very early stages where partners move from the attraction stage to a well-established partnership-like friendship; in the following chapter I shall examine the research on the growth from well-established partnerships to deep and intense relationships with special forms, like cohabitation, courtship, marriage and sexual relations. In the first case the major work concerns the intensification of feelings and the means by which people negotiate the adjustments that are required in their patterns of activity, their knowledge of one another, and their search for personality support. In the second case (chapter 4) the largest efforts of the partners are focused on changing the nature of the relationship, altering the public beliefs about the relationship, having it accepted by other people as an exclusive relationship, and negotiating the problems of satisfying physical needs as well as social ones.

In the present chapter we are dealing with matters that people readily overlook, unless they are pointed out strongly. When I ask people how they make friends, I hear them tell me *what* they talk about with strangers, but they overlook the really important things: *how* they talked about it all. Were the topics handled intimately? Did the topics make them embarrassed? If they shared opinions about some contentious issue, did their partner's opinions seem genuine or ingratiating? Were disagreements serious or playful? The manner in which such matters are dealt with is just as important as the topics themselves at this stage. Intimate topics such as sex handled in an offhand or flippant way do not convey the message that the conversation is caring, friendly, accepting or truly intimate. Casual topics discussed in a relaxed and friendly way do convey such messages. The point is that while the words concern the topic of conversation, the manner or style concerns, defines and exhibits the relationship between the speakers.

Another aspect of developing friendships which we easily overlook is the activities that we perform to develop them. People always focus on what they said to strangers, and they ignore that most crucial aspect: what they did next, and where they did it. Friendships do not start until people *do* friendly things in friendly places: they are not created merely by friendly talk. In fact the people have probably forgotten that they invited their new acquaintance or their new neighbour for a coffee or out to a bar for a drink, or they may have suggested going for a meal, visiting the local shops together, or going to a film. They may have liked what their acquaintance said, but until they have co-operated, socialised, fooled around, joked or accompanied one another somewhere they have only the bricks to build a relationship, but no foundation. In fact, once it is pressed, people usually come round to recognising or recalling that they did actually do such things and that these joint activities were what truly set the relationship going. Yet the activities are so easy to overlook and so easy to underestimate in importance that advice to lonely people hardly ever mentions them. Unfortunately, without attention to such matters no friendship can get very far off the ground.

The present chapter therefore deals closely with these topics. I shall focus on three main aspects of them. First I shall examine the ways in which acquaintances progressively attend to the attitudes of their partner both through word and action; second, I shall explore the means by which people increase their intimacy with one another and learn to reveal intimate information about themselves in proper and effective ways; lastly I shall deal with the recent research that has shown the overwhelming importance of the signals that friends must send out to the rest of the world about their new friendship. Together, these three areas comprise the early stages of development in acquaintance, the final resting place of many a friendship that might have been.

Getting Relationships Going: Seeking Similarity and Support

The main need of partners who are beginning acquaintance is for information about each other. This has to be imparted systematically, noticed when it is imparted, judged in relation to one's need for personality support, and treated publicly as useful and important. The second need is for the behaviour of friendship to be altered in a way that matches up with the partners' feelings for one another. This involves many major changes in the rule of conduct, in the matters that draw their attention and have significance, and in the expectations that the partners have about the future course of the friendship. The third need is for the creation of a pattern of communication that reflects their new relationship to each other. Formal, superficial styles of communication must be replaced with others that convey and adequately represent the level of intimacy that obtains in the relationship. Formal, stylised, unpersonalised ways of communicating about intimate matters, or during activities which are personal and intimate, are characteristic of instrumental relationships like prostitute-client ones. In proper, lasting, working relationships the style of communication and the activities must be made to correspond. Accordingly, the communication style must be monitored and developed as a part of the development of the relationship itself. Each of these three topics will be dealt with separately in the present chapter, although it is, of course, ultimately most important how they are combined.

Ask an ordinary person in the street what makes friendships work and you receive one of two contradictory answers. Some people assume that similarity is attractive ('Birds of a feather flock together'), whilst others assume that 'opposites attract'. In order to tidy up the confusion that these two contradictory, 'commonsense' ideas represent, a vast amount of work was carried out by research psychologists and demographers to try to find out which accounted best for friendship, courtship and marriage (see Duck, 1977 chapters 5 and 6). The research soon divided into three equal piles: one showing that similarity worked best, one showing that dissimilarity did, and one that neither of them worked at all. It is not hard to see why, and researchers were soon made aware of the fact that they were all looking at different things in the first place. What has to be similar or opposite? Similar heights? Opposite shoe sizes? Similar physical appearance? Opposite attitudes? For instance, it was found that friends are similar in attitudes, but courting couples are similar in their level of attractiveness (i.e. they do not necessarily look the same, but are about equally attractive). Married couples were found by other research to be opposite in major personality characteristics and showed 'complementarity of needs'. That is to say, married couples complement or fit one another's personality: a common finding would be, for instance, a dominant person married to a submissive one, or a helpful, initiative person married to a dependent one.

If we take the view outlined earlier about the need for

personality support then this all makes perfect sense. People need the reassurance of knowing that their partners share and accept many of their own attitudes and beliefs, but they also need to be interested, intrigued and even taught or challenged by their partner. One reason for not expecting people to want to be totally similar to their partner is that this would 'de-individuate' them, or make them lose their uniqueness. Friends could be expected to prefer to be very similar to one another in major attitudes and outlook, but to like to be different in other ways. What better ways to be different than in those that complement one another? Someone who likes to be led obviously needs to find the complementary person, a leader, as one of their steady life-partners. It seems perfectly understandable, then, that, as relationships proceed the persons will attempt to discover major similarities first, in order to give one another basic reassurance and security, but later on will try to look for differences. At the very early stages of friendship development, then, similarity is what counts and what should be demonstrated, revealed and displayed. A different strategy is needed later on, and I shall come to this in the next chapter.

Similarity of what, when? What sorts of similarity do intending friends, colleagues, workmates and lovers need to be good at showing at this stage? I have already mentioned in a previous chapter that the very first similarities that usually emerge are those that locate the partner: similarities of race, educational background and interests. At the next stage of developing friendship a different sort of similarity takes over and assumes a greater importance: basic similarity of attitudes and beliefs. One of the largest programmes of research in the last twenty years (Byrne, 1971; Przbyla and Byrne, 1981) has shown the deep and extensive ways in which similarity of attitudes influences the early development of relationships — including relatively swift and infrequent meetings between various professional groups and their clients. Bank managers, teachers, jurors and therapists have all been investigated in such research, alongside friends, lovers and married couples.

The basic finding is that the more similar two people's attitudes, the more they like one another (Byrne, 1971). Most effective is similarity in attitudes that the two partners believe to be most important to them, or which are rarely found in the population at large. A person who believes that the world is flat is particularly likely, therefore, to be attracted to someone else who holds the same belief. It is especially one that they wish to have supported and yet one that, by its very nature, rarely is: therefore another person who shares it is a godsend and will be highly attractive because of it. The initial stages of friendship development are thus characterised by active search for information about the other person's beliefs and attitudes. A major skill, therefore, consists in the ability to reveal one's attitudes in a way that gives the partner evidence about their importance and extent. A major demand, on the other hand, is for similar information from the partner and there are many techniques for opening up partners about their attitudes. The most obvious way is the direct question that asks for their view on a particular topic. This is risky, however, until one knows a little bit about how they might respond to such a question, since one wants to keep the topic as one where agreement is possible, if it is important. To announce your most preciously important belief without testing the possible response is to run the risk of having it rejected outright by the other person, who may not be perceptive enough to recognise its importance. A better strategy is to skirt around it, or to broach it in a gentle and tentative way, perhaps by the simple device of saying 'I know that some people believe that . . .', and seeing what the partner's response is like. A considerable amount of shadow-boxing goes on in these early encounters until the partners find a safe topic to agree on and use it as a base for excursions into more doubtful attitudinal territory (Miell, in preparation). In any case, a careful attention to the non-verbal signs of facial expression and tone of voice permits a person to learn more than is actually said in words. We can deduce someone's strength of feeling about a particular issue from careful observation of their posture, their hand movements and their breathing rate or facial colouring. By attending very carefully and thoughtfully to such clues it is possible also to work out the extent of someone's interest in a particular topic. Finally, from someone's general manner and demeanour when discussing attitudinal topics or matters of opinion, we can tell a lot about their personality style. We can learn about their openness to other views, their tolerance, their passions and flat spots, their dogmatisms and their assumptions about life. We can also learn a considerable amount about their attitudes to other people, to relationships and to the expression of feelings, as well as about their views on how other people should be treated. All this information is over and above what they tell us directly in words, but it helps us to see whether they are like us, and whether they offer the kind of personality style or support that we need.

It is not an easy task to be so attentive to other people's manner of discussing attitudes and beliefs; it takes work and effort to concentrate so fully not only on what they say, but on how they say it, and what that manner of delivery means about their inner 'clockwork'. Yet ultimately it is essential for the proper development of friendship and people can extend unnecessarily the length of time it takes to get to know someone if they are careless, inattentive or unskilled at this stage. By attending very carefully, they not only gather the sorts of information that they need about the other person's attitudes in order to structure their beliefs about their partner and to form useful expectations and predictions about the relationship, they also communicate interest and concern. Their partner will find this encouraging and is likely to reciprocate with a corresponding interest in the discussion.

To a research psychologist attitudes and personality are different concepts, and this may even be true for persons acquainting in real life. Attitudes are specific, value-laden statements about contentious issues; they are evaluations of probabilities or dogmatic views about large-scale political, religious or social issues. Personality, on the other hand, is the system in which attitudes are organised and the framework within which attitudes are expressed. Attitudes are the books in the personality library as it were, and just as books can be packed neatly and tightly in rows or left higgeldy-piggeldy, classified carefully, or just tossed anywhere, taken out and clustered for some special purpose, so it is with attitudes. They may be tightly or loosely organised according to the needs of the person who has them. Also, just as the library contains things other than books — such as the facilities that keep the reader warm and comfortable — so the personality 'contains' other things than attitudes. It consists also of needs, fears, hopes, ambitions; it comprises characteristic ways of doing things ('niceness', 'highhandedness') and a whole lot of other traits and modes of action. Accordingly, when we learn about someone's attitudes we learn an awful lot about what the personality contains, and how it is organised in some gross way — but there is still a lot to find out about (see next section). Nevertheless, attitudes give us knowledge of the basic outline, the peaks and troughs, of the partner's personality, and this is such a central goal of personal relationships that the effects of discovering attitude similarity are almost absurd in their extent. For instance Byrne (1971) has shown that bank managers give bigger loans to customers who are similar in attitudes. Juries recommend lighter sentences for defendants who have attitudes similar to those held by the jurors. Prejudiced whites give more favourable treatment to blacks with similar attitudes than to whites with dissimilar one, and so on.

These delightful peripheral findings of the research are sometimes disturbing, sometimes merely amusing and captivating. More significant in many ways are the findings in respect of teacher-pupil relationships and doctor-patient relationships. Several different studies have shown that teachers prefer and give more attention to pupils with attitudes similar to their own (e.g. Menges, 1969). For either this reason or the reason that the similarity improves communication between them, pupils learn more and faster from teachers who have similar attitudes, right the way up to very advanced levels. In the case of doctor-patient relationships, particularly psychotherapist-patient relationships, there has been shown to be an astonishing effect of attitudinal similarity upon the patient's recovery. Doctors and patients who get on well work better together and the patients recover sooner (Di Matteo, 1979). Not only this, but psychotherapists have a much lower success rate in dealing with patients who have dissimilar attitudes, and report that their patient was harder to get on with, had intractable problems, and was not truly committed to the treatment (Takens, 1982). It also seems probable that effectiveness in selling (e.g. selling insurance) is increased by sales personnel who can adopt the customer's attitude framework rapidly, and can stress similarities between themselves and the customer.

Disclosure of attitudes and a search for similarity is not merely a luxury in starting friendships: on the contrary, it serves a major function, and helps the partners to estimate the advantages of continuing or the benefits of closing down the development. The ability to reveal and assess attitudes is thus essential to the development of relationships, and consists largely of extensions of the skills described in the previous chapter, except that these are now focused on a different topic. The early signals about personality that are provided by the other person's attitudes are useful and quick, structured ways of communicating information about the person's inner life and structure of values. These provide major clues upon which to base the large changes in the behaviour of friendship that the partners also need to carry out in order to create the form and the type of relationship that they would like best.

Increasing Intimacy

Friendship is not just like a light bulb waiting for a person with the right characteristics to come and switch it on. The development of friendship occurs through the skills of partners in revealing or disclosing their attitudes first and later their personalities, inner character and true selves. This must be done in a reciprocal manner, turn-by-turn, and in a way that keeps pace with the revelations and disclosures made by the partner. The main feature that stabilises, establishes and develops relationships of all types is proper and dexterous control of *self-disclosure*; that is, the revelation of personal layers of one's self, personal thoughts, or even one's body (Jourard, 1971). In this last case, where self-disclosure can mean body disclosure, it is used to acknowledge the different access to our bodies that different people have. The better we know someone, the more we relax the complex rules governing the availability of our bodies, as the very metaphor of *close* friends suggest. For instance, we are 'permitted' to sit closer to people whom we know than to people whom we do not; we are 'allowed' to hold the hands or to touch the arms, shoulders or waists of close friends, but not of strangers; we are 'entitled' to wear informal clothes, to sprawl around, and to scratch ourselves when we are with friends rather than with people we do not know. Indeed, one definition of intimacy depends on 'what you scratch in front of whom and whose it is'! People sometimes do this inappropriately and cause offence.

A friend of mine used to irritate a lot of people simply by standing too close to them. They were unaware of what it was he was doing wrong that annoyed them, but when I pointed out that he was offering too much access to his body, they readily recognised that that was indeed the problem. Intimate friends expect close contact and physical closeness, expect to sit next to their friends, and so on. People who are mere acquaintances do not, and may feel hustled or overborne by someone who is too close. In tightly-packed lifts or tube trains we become distressingly aware of this, even though the contacts that we receive from the strangers there are ones we would expect and even enjoy from friends and people that we know well. To balance out the fact that we are touching strange people, we usually avoid looking them in the face — something we do not avoid with people we like. Since bodily closeness is such a powerful signal of intimacy it is something that must be carefully gauged in social relationships and should be tested out warily. Clever and deft relaters are good at light, quick touches on the arms, or perhaps they straighten someone's collar, or tap them lightly in a way intended to indicate what sort of feelings the partner has about being touched. If they move away, the touch was unwelcome, but otherwise a longer contact could be tried next time until the right level of closeness is established.

So self-disclosure is a key to relationship development because it applies to so many different features of relationships, each of which must be executed effectively. Although the physical kinds of disclosure are significant, the most important aspects undoubtedly concern disclosure of personality and inner self. Here the circumstances have to be appropriate: frank, open, honest disclosure is not always attracive. People who tell strangers exactly what they think are usually regarded not as open, honest and frank so much as rude, tactless and insensitive — yet exactly the same things can be said to a friend or to a doctor without being thought rude or tactless. The appropriateness or inappropriateness of disclosures is defined by the relationship between the two people and the level of intimacy that they seek to achieve.

Another aspect of self-disclosure that is important is that it should happen at all! Someone who never says anything about his personal opinions, inner thoughts, deeper feelings and intimate wishes will be cast aside as a closed, defensive and unrewarding person (Jourard, 1971). People like to know what their friend's intimate views are but more than this, they need to know, in order to find out about the person's true personality and the support that it can provide to their own. They also assume that someone who is open and disclosing is a mentally healthy person who has nothing to hide psychologically, and is balanced, mature and self-possessed. Some people never get this right, ranging from the person who clams up when personal topics come up in the conversation, to those who coolly disguise, dissemble and over-control their true feelings, right down to the person who is a toadying ingratiator, laughing at all the boss's unfunny jokes and going along with other people's opinions when he privately believes them to be wrong. Such people make it difficult for others to get to know them properly, and are often excluded from social relationships, or kept in only superficial ones for this very reason. Other people try to get their feelings across, but do it in an embarrassing or inappropriate way. For instance, they may insist on getting serious about a topic that everyone else was enjoying taking lightly. Or they may forever find that, whatever anyone says, they can turn the conversation around to something about themselves, or some opinion they will insist on going on about. In extreme cases they may just ignore what everyone else is talking about and keep droning on about themselves and their views of life, their own personal concerns or their present problems and anxieties. This has the same effect at this early stage of relationships of making other people draw back because the task of 'reading' the stranger's personality is made so awkward or because they are self-disclosing in the wrong way. They are easily dismissed as people with complex personality problems that make them unattractive company.

There are many other aspects of proper self-disclosure that will be discussed in the rest of this chapter. It will become clearer and clearer just how much self-disclosure matters to successful relationship growth for all sorts of reasons. These range from the fact that it gives people *direct* information about personality (whereas attitudes give only indirect hints), to the fact it also supplies indications of how far you trust them, and how fairly you 'balance up' by telling them as much about yourself as they tell you about themselves. Clearly, the more you tell them about your inner self, the more vulnerable you make yourself, and so the more trust and confidence in their loyalty you are therefore expressing.

Self-disclosure embodies many components, the first of which is clearly its communication aspect because it involves openly communicating about our personality and is the fastest means of establishing and developing personality support (Derlega and Chaikin, 1976). It would be unhelpful and confusing to reveal and communicate a whole personality in one giant disclosure, since the context for understanding its complexity has not been given. Accordingly, it has to be revealed bit by bit, stage by stage, layer by layer. Naturally this is where the first piece of craft comes in: knowing which part matters at what point in the relationship.

Our personality and our partner's personality are both made up of lots of different features which can be described in a variety of ways, and revealed in different forms. Practically everyone has their own idea about personality, and although the proper measurement of personality has become something approaching an exact science, popular ideas about it are vague and conflicting. Of course, we all tend to think of someone's personality as being 'extravert' or 'introvert', or some such split like that. However, we can also describe it as 'conforming / non-conforming', or 'generous / mean' and so on. There are scores and scores of more precise scientific systems of measurement. Naturally, someone can be both extravert and conforming, as well as generous, a Capricorn, impulsive, diplomatic, and resentful. It all depends on how an investigator decides to classify personality — whether he stops short at 'extravert' or at 'Capricorn'. More sophisticated views of personality suggest that there are very many ways to characterise the same person, and this is important because different parts of the personality come into play at different stages in a relationship's development (Duck, 1977, chapter 6). At the start of a relationship it matters how sociable someone is (i.e. whether that person is an introvert or an extravert) but later on, their sociability is less important than the way they conform and the way they think (e.g. whether they are rigid and dogmatic, or flexible and open-minded). Partners must self-disclose the relevant parts at the relevant places.

Second, it is not so much the 'true' personality of yourself and your partner that matters at the early stages so much as what you think or believe about each other's personality (Ajzen, 1977). In the early stages of relationships individuals make lots of guesses and inferences about the other person's personality and that is what starts to be very important. As discussed earlier in this chapter, attitudes constitute one major source of such guesses at the early stages. We are all looking for clues about our partner's personality. Longitudinal studies of developing relationships have shown the ways in which as the relationship develops, we start to look deeper (Duck, 1973, Duck and Craig, 1978). We probably do this unconsciously, like breathing, but occasionally we do it deliberately and in a measured way. Individuals try to find out more detail about their partner in order to assess whether their first impressions were accurate, or completely off the mark. As things proceed, so they get more information about the other person and can check their impressions for their accuracy or inaccuracy. The more they can get their partner to self-disclose, the easier is this job of checking first impressions, and if they are wrong (as they often will be) the easier it is to create newer, better impressions about the other person.

This is all very fine, but it implies that we know what to look for. It so happens that a lot of research shows conclusively that many people do not know what to look for, and so they do not develop relationships satisfactorily. One extreme example is provided by schizophrenics: they often do not understand other people's personalities in normal terms. For instance, they are likely to describe someone's personality — *personality* mind you — as 'tall / short' or 'heavy / light', and they seem to have no very good grasp of the psychological terms that the rest of us use like 'generous / mean', 'interested in other people / self-centred', or 'likes to control things / more relaxed'. If such persons do not know what a personality is, nor how best to understand it, then we can hardly expect that they will be able to form with other people those deep friendships that are based on personality judgements.

For those of us who do make reasonable sorts of assessment about other people's personality, our relationships will be successful the more accurate are our judgements — and both

71

accuracy and inaccuracy in judgement are learned for the first time in late childhood and early adolescence (see chapter 5). But they can be improved in adulthood by various means, such a psychotherapy, sensitivity group-training and various methods designed to increase awareness of other people's points of view, motivations, biases, moods and psychological structures — in short, their personality and psychological mainsprings. These methods are not particularly complicated, they merely focus people on something that they normally do not attend to especially closely. Some people do not spend long enough getting other people to talk about or share their feelings, and merely instructing them to think about this more carefully may do the trick.

There is another point to note — another side to the coin — in relation to assessments of personality. It is that we ourselves not only need to make assessments about the other person's self-disclosure, but must also help the other person to make assessments about us. This requires demonstration of our feelings, our biases, our motivations and our character through our behaviour.

To draw the moral from all this, we simply need to note that personality does not just affect relationship development in any simple, obvious way. Once more we come to the idea that it is what you *do* with it in friendship that makes it have any significance in making friendships grow. In this case what you do is to communicate your personality and get your partner to do the same thing. Both partners need to be able to get their views, opinions, preferences, needs and attitudes across — but they also need to ensure that their partner wants to hear them, and that they give the partner a fair chance to do the same. Developing a friendship does not mean monopolising the conversation; nor is it adequate merely to allow a prospective partner to do so either. Personality gets its importance in friendship from the manner in which it is displayed (choosing the right thing to display at the right moment), and from the 'decoding' of the personality of one's partner. We do this decoding partly through direct use of deliberate self-disclosure and partly through indirect, unintentional disclosures (Miell, *et al.*, 1979).

If these two points are added together, we end up with a much more sophisticated and practically useful idea about what is going on in relationship growth. The advice about improving relationships and relationship growth is consequently given a more sensible foundation. Instead of suggesting that people have face-lifts, haircuts and new clothes or take up new hobbies or join clubs, we end up pointing to a range of judgements and indirect disclosures that may need to be practised or 'trained up' in people whose relationships are presently unsatisfactory. It is easy to rehearse these skills privately, without formal training, although intractable cases need special guidance. But what skills and what indirect disclosures? Let us assume that the non-verbal behaviour mentioned in chapter 2 (eye movements, posture, gesture and so forth) is adequately mastered in the ways described earlier. That is, let us assume that the person knows that smiles and eye movements, for example, are important as indicators of general interest in the other person, and that they use them appropriately. We can now take this a step further and show that these same things fit into the more advanced kinds of disclosing activity required in developing satisfying relationships.

Smiles, nods and eye movements in appropriate places do not serve only to show general interest, nor just to stress important points in conversation, nor even to keep the conversation going: they have a fourth, separate function — they indicate aspects of our personality. We are called 'rude' if we do not look at someone when they are talking to us, although we hear with our ears wherever our eyes are looking. Equally it is rude to stare, that is, to look at a person too much or too long. So such non-verbal behaviours also show that we know the proper rules of polite conversation, and we are not abnormal or deranged. So we have to look at people when we are nearing the end of what we want to say, but look away when we have not finished and do not want to be interrupted; we have to use flicks of the eyes to indicate that we are saying something important, and so on. These and many, many other cues are used in order to conduct our social activities appropriately.

My point is simply that the rules are sometimes broken or used inappropriately. People who interrupt when we talk are thought to have 'rude' personalities, people who do not talk when the conversation pauses for them are called 'socially inept'; people who monopolise the conversation are called 'boring'. Equally, people who do not make the normal use of eye movements to indicate the main points, or the boundaries of their conversation, are hard to cope with. These people tend to become isolated simply because others cannot cope with them: they do not give the right signals, we do not know whether they are interested or not, and we cannot tell much about their personality. Accordingly, we do not know whether we are giving them the right information, and whether our indications about our own personality have been helpful to them or not. Equally, it will probably be hard to get them to disclose the relevant things about themselves because we cannot properly conduct a conversation that makes it possible to draw them usefully out of themselves. For instance, if I am only prepared to talk about the weather then no one will learn much about my personality, except that it is narrow, closed and unintriguing. Yet if I talk about the most crucial decisions I have ever had to make, or things I am ashamed of in my past life, then my personal feelings are being brought out more obviously. My priorities, my values, my hopes and fears are all being exposed to the other person's view. Naturally, normal people open themselves up more and more as their relationships grow and they are prepared — at the right sort of moments, and in the right circumstances — to reveal more and more about these personal thoughts.

So another key aspect of self-disclosure is the management of the intimacy level of what we reveal (Cozby, 1973). Usually, researchers examine the information that people disclose about themselves and whether or not it is intimate. For instance, they may look at the extent to which a person talks about private thoughts, feelings about personal matters, and intimate experiences. If they do so, do they do it at the right times and in the right ways, or are they always telling perfect strangers the sorts of private details that strangers don't really want to know? The research has shown two main aspects to this: the pacing of the deepening of intimacy, and the timing of negative/positive information about yourself (Chelune, 1979). Increasing intimacy of disclosure is a key problem in developing normal friendships because the intimacy and privacy of disclosed information has to be increased steadily so that you reveal more and more about the deeper and more private aspects of your personality. These parts are precisely the ones that are most important for your partner to test out as providers of support for his or her own personality. However, the person who discloses too intimately too soon is likely to be thought peculiar, indiscreet or untrustworthy. On the other hand, the person who tries to get *you* to disclose too intimately will be thought driving and pushy, unless there are special reasons why they are doing it (e.g. a doctor or a therapist are people who are 'allowed' to push).

The other aspect of pacing intimacy that must be right is the timing of negative / positive information about oneself. American researchers have shown that people are disliked if they disclose positive information about themselves early in a relationship, but not if it comes later (Jones and Gordon, 1972). Negative information should be disclosed early, however, if the person caused it themselves (e.g. if the negative information is some misfortune they brought upon themselves by heedlessness). Evidently people are attracted to someone who seems willing to own up to responsibility early on — but someone whose negative information is to do with bad luck which is not their own fault should keep quiet about it as long as possible! What this research shows is that people are less influenced by the positive or negative aspect of the information itself, than by the timing of its disclosure and the manner in which it is done. (The same goes for evidence in court: research (Frankel and Morris, 1976) has shown that if a defendant has positive information about himself to tell the court he should get someone else to tell it. In controlled experiments using exactly the same bit of information, defendants who told it themselves to a mock jury got harsher sentences than defendants who had an independent outsider tell it for them.)

So pacing of self-disclosure helps us to find out about each other in a systematic way. It also assists us by controlling the amount of information that is available to us at a given time and so does not overload our minds with things that are too detailed to understand: it gives us time to absorb it systematically. Finally, such rules of disclosure again tell us something fundamental when they are *in*competently done: there is a whole range of rather negative judgements that will be heaped on a person who does not do this 'right'. Not only, as has been said, will someone who is too free with personal information probably be labelled bizarre or even mad; more significantly, we are likely to assume that he tells everyone such things, and we shall not assume he is telling is to us particularly because he likes us personally. So we shan't treat it as indicating a wish for a friendship with us personally; we shall treat it as indicating indiscretion.

Just as necessary as the fact that we reveal things about ourselves, pace it correctly, and observe the usual 'rules', is that we should reciprocate what the partner does. If a person reveals something intimate, then it is attractive when their partner reveals something equally intimate — not necessarily about the same topic, but something at the same depth of intimacy. If a person asks direct questions about some particular area of personality then it helps to develop the friendship if the partner invites him to disclose that area of his personality too. If someone shows reluctance to talk about a particular sort of topic then it is better not to question and probe directly. Indirect reference should be made to one's own feeling on the topic or a similar one so that he is encouraged to reciprocate and will feel less vulnerable.

Self-disclosure is still a major topic of research and there is much about it that we do not know. However, many unexpected things have been found out (Miell *et al.*, 1979). For one thing, there are very clear differences between the two sexes when we look at the amounts of intimate information that are disclosed to a partner. Females disclose more intimate information to their partners than males do, for instance. It does not seem to matter whether the partner is a male or a female: females are simply more open than males.

Various explanations have been offered for this highly consistent finding. At one extreme are those theorists who stress the cultural pressure on women to be more 'relationship-oriented', and be more personal, intimate and open in relationships, whilst men are encouraged to retain a 'masculine' aloofness from personal relationships. Another sort of explanation assumes that women are less competitive than men and do not worry so much about becoming vulnerable in relationships by exposing their more personal thoughts. A third possibility is that women are implicitly taking the initiative in offering the chance to form a better relationship by presenting the building-blocks at an earlier point than men do.

Whichever of these — and several other — explanations is correct, it is certain that people of both sexes expect women to disclose themselves more than men do, and that those women who do not do so will risk dislike, rejection and avoidance. This is particularly the case in dating and courtship, where men tend to take involuntary control of disclosure by asking more direct questions than the women do — usually also more intimate and probing questions (Davis, 1978). By contrast, women lead by example — that is, they disclose personal information in the expectation that the man will reciprocate. Men are attracted to a female partner who responds suitably, but they do not like one who attempts to avoid the question, or answers it with information less intimate than was expected. Equally, men do not like to be probed too early themselves — whether by women or by other men — and many a promising relationship has been uprooted by a male's negative reaction to a too-questioning partner.

However undesirable such sex differences may be, it is clear that they represent some strong cultural norms at work. The effects are so widespread — being reported in USA, Great Britain and Europe — that they are clearly ingrained in our present cultural make-up, and yet represent such a subtle difference that it is unlikely that more people are conscious of them. They do react negatively when the 'rules' are broken and it is likely that considerable effort would be needed in schools and other places of cultural learning before equality of disclosure expectation can be achieved.

The more recent research, by Dorothy Miell at Lancaster (Miell, in preparation), indicates that people use self-disclosure strategically in getting to know other people. Skilful friend-makers are careful to choose their moment for probing a particular area of personality or behaviour or attitudes. They wait to see how the partner responds, they throw in a comment of their own that helps the partner to reciprocate. They press into new areas swiftly when they want to force the pace a bit, but quickly withdraw for a while before probing into it again more gently. Rather than producing a steady pressure on a particular area, they seem to use a sort of battering-ram approach — push, withdraw, wait; push harder, draw back, wait; push further, and so on.

But just as such people make skilful use of self-disclosure so, conversely, the people who have most difficulty with normal friendship development seem to be least adept at this part of it. People can be trained to get self-disclosure right partly by guided exercises that indicate the different depths of information that are appropriate at different stages of relationships, and partly by putting them in a warmly accepting atmosphere that encourages them to open up about such things. It is important to focus on this because the person who self-discloses inadequately or inappropriately is likely to be labelled negatively, to be avoided, and eventually to be cast out — perhaps without anyone ever telling him why. The processes here are subtle, so that people may not be *able* to tell why — it is difficult to verbalise — and indeed there are also strong social taboos that prohibit discussion of such things. It is very difficult to break the liking taboo and look someone straight in the eye whilst saying then that you like them, for example. Except in dates, where 'I love you' is an accepted gambit, we are supposed not to express ourselves so directly. We are supposed to do it more subtly by non-verbal means — by smiles, friendly looks, evident happiness and enjoyment of the other person's company.

Equally, we are not supposed to talk directly about the way someone behaves. Even though best friends can tell you about BO, they would find it hard to say, 'Do you realise everyone thinks you are shifty because you never look them in the eye?' It is very hard to tell someone that he is a social clam or a bore because he gets self-disclosure wrong. Even if someone is inept enough to ask you if he is boring you, it is either a brave person or a rude one who will give the straight answer 'Yes', and take the social consequences. For these reasons it is very unusual and often very difficult for people to draw attention to someone's self-disclosing habits and to cope with the social and emotional disruption that follows. If you don't believe me, just try doing it. People do respond very fiercely when this taboo is broken, often without being able to say why. They just know they can't relate to someone who doesn't do it right.

So the satisfactory development of a relationship will depend on the 'proper' use of self-disclosure and personality communication. That is to say, in the present cultural climate, men will tend to take the lead by encouraging females to disclose, but they will not disclose so much themselves; females are expected (even unfairly pressurised) to disclose more information at an earlier point in an acquaintance than males are. People look for reciprocation, for proper pacing, and for deepening intimacy of disclosure.

Also, the circumstances must be right: in some situations it is not permissible to disclose what not only would be right but would probably be expected in other circumstances. The classic example of this is in the job interview, where very personal information is often sought in a direct way that would be regarded as highly offensive in other circumstances — for instance, in talking to a stranger in a pub, or in talking to acquaintances at work (unless they were new arrivals, who are generally regarded as fair game for interrogation).

It is obvious, however, that most of the emphasis of this notion of self-disclosure falls upon the way that people think, the words that they use, the information that they reveal — mostly, that is, on the abstract, intangible things that relate to thought and intellectual activity. For all of these reasons, self-disclosure is of great help to people in developing personal relationships, and its proper use allows individuals to assess the amount of personality support they can offer one another — but to do this in a systematic, programmatic and efficient way.

Showing that the Relationship is Growing

As indicated earlier, though, there is more to developing satisfying relationships than merely extracting the abstract items that help them to grow. Their growth must be indicated in behaviour, and they must be maintained. In this section I shall look at the research which shows how activity changes as relationships grow, indeed, how it must change. Later, I shall consider the effects of 'publishing' a relationship in this way, particularly as it affects the rest of the social group that the partners belong to. The attitudes and responses of the group are often very influential in the development of relationships, particularly as they get very close.

Researchers have been loath to look at what people actually do in friendship for fear that the research will interfere with the relationship, and it is only recently that such studies of human social behaviour have really got off the ground (Hinde, 1979; 1981; McCarthy, 1981). Indeed, we found out a lot more about what monkeys and ants actually do in relationships than we did about real life humans — except humans in the sterilised, scientific laboratory, and they don't always behave the way they normally would.

One reason for this surprising omission is because everyone tended to assume that they knew what people did, and so did not need to make records or do observations. It is not surprising, then, that there were several shocks in store for us all when the job of cataloguing social behaviour was begun. For instance, if we were asked what distinguishes the husband-wife relationship from all others in terms of reported activities done together, then most of us would expect something to do with sex to make the top of the list. In fact sexual activity does not distinguish husband-wife pairs from many other sorts of couple (Argyle, 1981). The activity that separates married couples from everyone else is that they spend more time watching TV together!

Joint activity is more than just fun: it serves an accepted social signalling purpose. Quite simply it helps to indicate — both to the partners and to the rest of the world — that the partners are friends, and although friendship is based on feeling, the feelings have to be demonstrated, or else people will not know that the feelings are there. Equally, people have to change what they do together as the relationship grows, since this is a necessary means of showing that the friendship is developing and changing too. In some countries there used to be a very clear example of this when the partners formally agreed to switch from the distant form of address ('Vous' in French, 'Sie' in German) to the intimate form ('Tu' in French, 'Du' in German). Even in our own language system the same person may be called 'Sir', 'Mr Jones', 'Robert', 'Bob' or 'You old bastard', depending on the degree to which we are getting to know him personally.

The pattern and diversity of interactions, joint activity and shared pursuits will also gradually alter as a friendship grows. Not only will the partners do more together and spend a higher percentage of their time in one another's company, they will also tend to do different things together (Hinde, 1981). For instance, people may originally meet at work, and so pattern their meetings within certain particular hours of the day, talking about a relatively narrow set of topics (e.g. the foreman, the job, the news in the day's papers) and doing a very restricted set of things together (e.g. eating lunch together, chatting). As the relationship grows so they may meet outside work, at different times of day or evening, do a wider range of things together (e.g. playing sport, going to the cinema) and talking about a wider range of issues. Many other aspects of their activities also change (Hinde, 1981). For instance the intensity of the actions will increase: where they used to kiss tenderly they will now kiss passionately; where they used to smile politely they will now smile affectionately; where they used to laugh dutifully they will now laugh from genuine joy or happiness.

Furthermore, there are important consequences of the fact that friendship is not merely something abstract or some rarified feeling. It is a way of acting; it is a way of behaving. It is here that we can usefully revisit the idea earlier in the chapter about complementarity; the idea that dominant people marry submissive ones, that people work well together when they have complementary skills. This is where it actually matters: when people actually behave towards one another. If two friends can work out complementary ways of behaving towards each other then they will create a good working friendship.

Consider two people sharing a flat: if both persons actually enjoy doing the washing up and neither likes to hoover the carpet then not only will they fight about who washes up, but also they will soon be ankle deep in cigarette ash. However, if they can work out a complementary system where they each take turns at each job then things will run smoothly. So it is in the sharing of a friendship. If both partners like to run the friendship it will get out of control, but if they can work out a bit that each of them 'runs' it will go well. Under these sorts of circumstance complementarity is attractive; otherwise it is not. But in any case it involves work, discussion and give-and-take. The partners have to negotiate and create a complementary system for their friendship as it develops; these things do not just happen. Doing the necessary negotiation is one of the very complex skills of friendship development that need a lot of thought and practice.

Because of these negotiations and these necessary alterations to activity and because they mean, demonstrate, clarify things about two persons' relationship to one another, people come to expect them as signs of the growth of their friendship. They become distressed, annoyed or hurt if the patterns of activity in the relationship do not seem to change in a fashion that indicates a growing relationship. So it is important to *demonstrate* affection and feeling once friendships are begun, both directly by verbal means and indirectly through non-verbal behaviour or changes in type of shared and negotiated activity.

Conversely, people indicate to one another their willingness or their reluctance to become more intimate and allow the relationship to grow. In some cases there are various normative forces that help here: there are quite wide ranges of tolerance for the friendliness or openness with which they may be conducted. For instance, teachers and pupils may behave in a very friendly way to one another — be on first name terms, for example — or be very very distant and formal. Whichever is true, there are very strict sanctions that would be employed if the two became lovers, sanctions which would not be applied to two unmarried persons who worked in the same office.

When the situation itself is less prominent and forceful, people have to let one another know the limits that they perceive to the relationship, whether they see it as likely to grow, whether they want it to do so, and so on. Some people are uncomfortable when relationships get more intimate, and prefer to keep them distant and superficial. They feel they will lose control over the relationship as their feelings get stronger and so they draw sharply back or indicate non-verbally that they want room, distance, space. How then do these desires and their opposites get indicated and communicated? The answer is subtly rather than directly.

Whenever someone shows himself to be keen to enter a relationship, he is risking himself and making himself vulnerable. If someone asks directly 'Will you be my friend?', then he risks the straight answer 'No'. Such an undesired answer will obviously be threatening and offensive. Thus, except in very special circumstances (e.g. in making a proposal of marriage), people do not ask directly, but make the indications subtly and, usually, by non-verbal means or through style of behaviour. For instance, the wish to become closer can be shown by indicating greater interest in the person, by showing that you enjoy their company, by confiding, by asking for personal advice and seeking opinions, or generally creating more opportunities for further meetings in a wider variety of circumstances. When the invitation is thus indicated obliquely, indirectly and ambiguously, it may be acknowledged or ignored without offence. For example, if someone asks a partner for advice about a private or personal matter, then the 'target' can treat this either as a move towards friendship and reply in a confiding or intimate way, or as a neutral matter by replying in a detailed but matter-of-fact way, or merely as a business matter for which the advice is given very formally and in a distant tone.

This social fact has several implications: first, we often may not realise what the other person intended until later. Second, some people will be better and some worse at detecting the subtle differences that are possible in such responses. So some will take and others miss opportunities simply because of their different abilities to detect — detect fast enough, that is — what their partner is intending. Third, some people will be better and some worse at putting their own intentions across in suitably subtle ways: as the Beatles once said of the Fool on the Hill, 'Nobody seems to like him, they can see what he wants to do.' Intentions or desires that are too explicit can be offensive or simply amusing, and there are many more subtle ways in which people avoid direct or explicit expression of them. They cut down both the risks and the offence by making characteristic changes in the 'contents' of what they do in relationships and in the ways in which they communicate about it. Such changes in the patterns and diversity of their activities, the frequency of their meetings and their communication styles are all ways of indicating, cementing and establishing increases in intimacy and commitment and they convey the same desires and intentions, but do so in a safer and socially more acceptable way.

The most recognised way of doing this is by altering the 'currency' of the relationship (La Gaipa, 1977). In all meetings with other people, various tangible or intangible rewards are exchanged. To take a simple example, if I go into a shop I may buy a tie and give money for it: I receive the 'reward' of the tie and the shop assistant receives the 'reward' of money. Or I may go to an evening class to learn about basket weaving, in which case I receive the reward of information in exchange for a part of my enrolment fee. Or I may win a difficult sales order and be promoted to director on the spot, receiving the reward of status for the service of marketing. Social psychologists have long conceived of social behaviour in terms of rewards and exchange of resources, as indicated briefly in chapter 1. Whether or not one accepts that the general principles apply to established intimate relationships, it is clear that developing relationships can usefully be seen in terms of the economic analogy. As the relationship grows, so there are systematic changes in the economy of the relationship (Hatfield and Traupmann, 1981).

For one thing, the type and value of the rewards change (La Gaipa, 1977). Friends do not spend most of their time exchanging goods for money: they are more likely to swap information for information, services for services, or love for love. In short, they move away from concrete items as the predominant content of their activity, and instead spend more time on the abstract. The quality of the rewards changes in personal terms also: money has the same value whoever gives it to you, but love is valued (or not) as a result of the person who offers it. Finally, as relationships become deeper there is less concern over immediate repayment of rewards: while casual acquaintances are concerned not to do too much for each other without being rewarded in return, close friends are more likely to be prepared to do favours without expecting instant 'payment'. Part of the key development of friendship thus concerns the extension of the timespan for the return or reciprocation of rewards. Someone who is always keeping score about who owes whom what will be difficult to relate to, and his insistence on acting in a manner consistent with only casual acquaintance will make it hard for the partner to feel any closer. This is quite simply because he is acting in a way that is not consistent with the growth of the relationship and the changing definition of the relationship as expressed in its exchange or reward pattern.

Another major way of indicating change in the relationship is through change in the patterns of communication within it (Morton and Douglas, 1981). A simple change at the developmental stage is that partners begin to communicate more vigorously about attitudes and beliefs. The change from discussion of 'locating information' (as in chapter 2) to attitudes, values and beliefs is thus one subtle alteration to the communication structure in the relationship and one that, in properly conducted relationships, rapidly gives way to disclosures about personal feelings and the deeper aspects of personality. Partners at this stage of all relationships begin to share more interpretations of life and to communicate at a level that consists of personal judgements and values.

However, the pattern of communication changes not only in terms of its subject matter but also in terms of its style (Morton and Douglas, 1981). Not only does formality decrease as the partners become more familiar with one another, but relaxation of rules of behaviour is accompanied by a greater openness and a greater willingness to share secrets. Private stories about the past are shared, and the partners make their weaknesses and mistakes as much a part of the debate as their strengths and successes. This serves to make each person more vulnerable, of course, since each partner begins to build up a picture of the other person's private life, the things they dislike about themselves, and their errors or omissions or past failures. However such vulnerability is usually reciprocal because both partners expose themselves in this new communication style. It serves to bind them together and to increase commitment to the relationship, therefore, and is very important to the development of the relationship.

The purpose of many of the communicational changes that occur is indeed to set up a new structure of assumptions in the relationship. As the relationship grows, so partners communicate more about their shared past rather than their separate pasts. This often involves them talking about their feelings about some shared experience and has the consequence of making them focus on the relationship itself and their feelings about it. It thus promotes an agreed definition of the relationship and its form, which is essential for its growth. Partners need to work towards an agreed definition of the future of the relationship, and to set up shared expectations about its ultimate shape. In my own studies of dating couples, one of the most frequent reasons for breaking up was that the two partners had different expectations about the relationship. 'It was getting to intense. My partner wanted more from it than I was prepared to give just yet', was a very frequent type of response. By communicating about the relationship, its past, its future and its probable length, the partners help to create an agreed picture of it that helps them to shape and stabilise it.

A further unconscious consequence of such talk is that it increases the partner's feelings of security in the relationship, enhances their commitment to the partner, and their beliefs about the partner's commitment, raises or creates trust, and strengthens the stability of the relationship. By stressing the links between the partners in both the past and future, it also raises their feelings of relatedness or interdependence, and hence serves an important function in increasing intimacy in the relationship. But the growth in intimacy stems from the structural and stylistic changes in communication just as much as from any changes in the content of their conversation.

These changes in the economy of the relationship, in the activity patterns, and in the communication styles matter most to the two partners themselves in defining their relationship, but the changes also have another function. They indicate *to outsiders* that the relationship has been formed. Outsiders can interpret the non-verbal signals between people, the communication changes, and the change of prespective just as well as the insiders can. Outsiders can often tell when two people are in love from the way that they behave in public, even when they do not know them.

This is all obvious enough, but it is important because outsiders exert an influence on relationship development and, in some cases, can influence the form that it eventually takes — the father with a shotgun being the clearest example. For most partners it is important to gain other people's acceptance of their new friend, date, lover, spouse or companion, not only as a person but as '*my* friend', '*my* date', and so on. In short, the partners need the seal of approval that their other friends and associates can provide. Studies consistently show, for example, that parental approval is positively related to marital adjustment: when parents fully accept the marriage partner, that marriage is a happier one. In general, such approval helps to prevent break up of the marriage and speeds up the prospects of the relationship during its formative period. Nevertheless, there is a study showing that where such approval is withheld in dating, the partner actually becomes more attractive to the person. The now famous 'Romeo and Juliet effect' was first found in a study of parents' reactions to dating partners which showed that parental disapproval very often pushed the partners closer together rather than further apart (Driscoll, *et al.*, 1972). In other cases, particularly in teenage gangs, a new date has to be approved by the whole group, and a person risks losing membership of the gang if he chooses a partner who is not so approved. It can come down to a simple choice between the new partner and the gang, and he must give up one or the other.

In making a relationship and making it develop, therefore, the partners will be subject to group influences and pressures, particularly in the case of intimate relationships, to which we now turn.

Summary

This chapter has emphasised the changes in information and activity patterns that characterise developing relationships. I have focused on attitudes, opinions, beliefs, personality and the actions that people perform in relationships. I stressed at the beginning that we never know what is really going on in other people's minds, and we need clues from their actions. Thus attitudes and opinion statements have great significance at the early stages of development of a relationship because they give neatly packaged signals about the more mysterious parts of a partner's inner life. Later, the force of self-disclosure becomes powerfully attached to these very mysterious private feelings and desires themselves because, in self-disclosure, people convey personal information so directly. As feelings for each other increase, so partners must begin to signal this important fact much more to each other. They do this by changing their activity patterns, their communication style, and the 'economy' of their relationship — that is, the way they exchange goods, favours, help, and so on. Such changes also serve to alert outsiders to the fact that the new relationship exists. So it serves to draw the two partners into the wider social system that must sanction and approve the creation of the new partnership.

4

Taking it Further

In the previous chapter I was exploring the means by which relationships are intensified, paying particular attention to the changes in behaviour and communication patterns that occur. Many types of relationship begin in the ways described, but then start to take different forms, or to branch into avenues not possible in the other relationships. These changes are sometimes quite dramatic and bring their own problems, requiring large adjustments from one or both partners. For instance, when dating couples decide to get married they have to cope with the changes to their relationship that follow; they have to adjust to the implications that the new relationship will have. For example, marriage is a socially recognised relationship, with legal and contractual implications; partners will now live together for the foreseeable future; they will possibly be regarded as failures if they do not do it successfully; they might prepare to have a family, and so on. The changes may bring rewards, but also have to be coped with, as well as having to be brought about and created successfully when desired.

In other relationships, too, there are other sorts of change that fundamentally restructure the partners' beliefs about each other and require a considerable amount of thought and adjustment if they are to be coped with well. Partners may decide to cohabit, or may decide to engage in sexual intercourse; a couple might decide to start a family; parents may have to face up to their children leaving home; a person may retire from his place of work and leave all the relationships that he had enjoyed there. All of these decisions or events have consequences for the partners and for the relationship, all of which have to be negotiated and carried out systematically and skilfully. Once they are coped with, the person's life has to be set back in balance and adjustments in attitudes towards the partner or to feelings about the relationship have to be set in frame again, against the background of the new developments. Because of their importance to the lives of the people involved, research has focused strongly on such changes, and the proper ways of accomplishing them have been scrutinised. Evidently they involve a different range of skills from the earlier ones and a range that, even when carried out efficiently, can still produce stress. High stress scores on the so-called 'significant life events scale' are associated with the decision to marry, to set up a house, or to start a family, as well as arising from divorce, death of a spouse, and loss of children who leave home. In most people's lives these relationship events are exacting and in need of careful understanding.

One hidden factor in all of these changes stems from the fact that people have to respond to a hidden pressure that lurks in relationships. Like a germinating seed, the beginning of some relationships is not only rich in promise and hope, but is also pregnant with a whole range of detailed, programmed expectations about the shape and form of the relationship that will eventually be created — if everything goes according to plan. Even when the plan is effectively and smoothly carried out, it involves the partners in many kinds of change in activity and in beliefs about themselves, as well, perhaps, as changes in status, responsibility, and duties (as when newly-married couples buy a house, for example). Despite the increasing demands that this may create upon them, the partners are more likely to feel satisfied with the relationship when its implied 'programme' is completed exactly as expected. On the other hand, when it is carried out too quickly (as in whirlwind romances) the partners may have too little time to make the necessary adjustments, or to create the essential kinds of patterns of activity that the new form of relationship entails. If the relationship's programmed demands are carried out too slowly or not realised at all (for instance, when long-term dating couples realise that one of them does not really intend to marry the partner) then the partners also experience distress — even when the relationship is perfectly happy in its present form. The problem is not necessarily that the relationship itself is unsatisfactory or unenjoyable, but that it does not match up to expectations: the unhappy comparison of reality with hopes is what causes the difficulty. In my own studies a frequent way of expressing this feeling was to say 'The relationship was lovely, but it wasn't going anywhere'.

When people embark on certain sorts of relationships there are very often highly specific expectancies built into the whole arrangement. For instance, the couple may have the expectancy that they will eventually marry. If it becomes clear that this is going to be delayed, or if one partner seems unwilling to take the plunge, then the relationship becomes pointless, even if it is still enjoyable. Indeed, many courtships break up at around 15-18 months in, just because one of the partners becomes dissatisfied with the rate of progress towards the expected state; and if the relationship will not change, then it must die.

In other cases the implicit demands in the relationship concern certain kinds of activity that partners would expect to enjoy together. For example, friends would expect to share more private details and secret knowledge, and to do a wider variety of activities together as their relationship grows deeper; or they may expect to have sex at some later stage. In these cases the problem centres on the ways to bring the changes about at the most agreeable and suitable times, as well as about the most satisfactory manner to execute the decision. In former days such decisions were often structured for a couple: sex first took place on the wedding night, often in the presence of a group of witnesses. Nowadays such activity is usually negotiated in private and can occur at other times or in other forms of relationship. Researchers have recently begun to look at the ways in which such decisions are taken. I shall look at the research on such decisions, starting with partners' decisions to engage in sexual intercourse or to cohabit. However, other decisions and other changes are also important in relationships later in life; for instance, the decision to move from being a 'married couple' to being a 'family', and the change from 'family' to 'empty nesters' when grown up children leave home. I shall look at those later in the present chapter, and shall focus particularly on the skills of coping with the changes, as well as the means of bringing them about.

Researchers have for a long time been interested in the instigation of premarital sexual intercourse, and have identified several influential factors in isolation (Cate and Christopher, 1982). Approval and frequency of premarital sexual intercourse are statistically related to such things as religious beliefs, pervious sexual experience, age at first intercourse, and the sexual behaviour of friends or people in the surrounding networks or friendship groups. None of these statistical findings tells us what we really need to know, however. What researchers have tried recently to discover is the process by which individuals decide to start a sexual involvement with a partner before marriage. What do people weigh up in their minds when they are deciding such a question, and what influences sway their decisions?

In a very recent study (Cate and Christopher, 1982), where investigators looked at this question, they found that there were basically four things that had mattered to people in their decision:

(i) *The positive feelings* that partners had for one another, and whether they had discussed these feelings together. For instance, couples who loved one another more and felt more committed to each other were more likely to have discussed their feelings and to have considered the meaning of intercourse for their relationship. If they decided that the meaning of sexual intercourse for the relationship was one that had positive overtones for both of them, gave them a sense of increased commitment, and set the relationship further along the track towards marriage, then they were more likely to have decided for intercourse.

(ii) *The two partners' arousal.* The second most important influence was, naturally enough, found to be the state of excitement, anticipation or arousal before the relevant date where intercourse occurred and also physical arousal during the date. Partners who felt strong commitment but were not aroused physically simply postponed the activity of intercourse until a later occasion, as one might expect. It is interesting to note that many primitive tribes engage in considerable physical exertion and try to create high arousal and excitement through dance, music, games and ritual exercising during fertility rites which traditionally end in intercourse. Violent physical exercise and

dancing can create the necessary state of arousal for intercourse.
(iii) *Obligation and pressure.* A third feature in the decision was
the amount of obligation or pressure exerted by one's partner,
one's friends, one's partner's friends, and oneself. The res-
pondents in the investigation often reported that they were
reacting to pressures like this, although it is very likely that such
pressure actually also comes from the demands created by the
expectations in the relationship. Some relationships between
young people (and even older ones) have a strong pressure for
intercourse in them, partly as 'initiation rites', and partly
because it is 'what everybody does' in such relationships.
Adjustment to these pressures is often a distressing problem for
some couples, who respond to the demands rather than to their
own personal wishes. This is particularly true of the males who
were interviewed, many of whom reported significantly more
pressure from their friends to have intercourse with the most
recent dating partner.
(iv) *Circumstances.* A larger number of the interviewees reported
that premarital intercourse was a result of circumstantial factors, like the availability of drugs or alcohol, the fact that the
relevant date was a really special event, and so on.

The two sexes respond differently to these four inducements,
with females reporting a much greater influence of 'positive
feelings' in their decision than the males did. Inexperienced
individuals also reported that feelings mattered more than any
of the other forces, whereas sexually-experienced persons were
more influenced by arousal level than by anything else.

This study makes it perfectly clear that decisions about the
first moves in a sexual involvement are not a simple matter. On
the contrary, the decisions involve many kinds of pressures and
considerations, some of which stem from the nature of the
relationship, some from expectations about where it will lead,
and some from unpredictable circumstances. As such relationships mature, and in other relationships where the decision is
implicit (such as marriage), the problem shifts from the initial
decision and onto the management of sexual desires, patterns
and frequency of intercourse, and so on. To a very large extent
such relationships will be successful or unsuccessful as a direct
result of the partners' abilities and skills in creating the desired
patterns of activity, in this respect as in respect of other activities

in other relationships. Most people nowadays reject the naïve idea that sexual relationships are purely physical events, and research continually demonstrates the truth of the alternative view that they are *relationships* (Yaffé, 1981). As such they reflect the rest of the relationship like a barometer. Sexual difficulties and sexual problems as often stem from relationship problems as from other causes. Contrariwise, relationship stress follows sexual difficulties. In studies of American couples (reported in Markman, *et al.*, 1982) it has been found that three out of every five women and two out of every five men who were dissatisfied with their marriage reported no pleasure from sexual activity for about a year before they complained about their marriage. This correlation between sexual dissatisfaction and dissatisfaction with the marriage is found in newlyweds as much as in people who have been married for up to twenty years. It seems that sexual adjustment and marital adjustment are strongly related and the correlation provides further evidence for the point that I made in the previous chapter: the quality of a relationship, whether friendship, courtship, marriage or work, depends very largely upon the quality of the activities that take place within it. Feelings and activities are not independent: feelings about the partner come from the activities that are performed together — or, more importantly, come from the way that people look at what they do together. If they see themselves enjoying one another's company, they believe more firmly that they like one another. When the activities are enjoyable, feelings about the partner reflect that; when they are not, the feelings change. It is not as simple as we used to believe: that the feelings dictate the activities that we perform; the reverse is equally true.

The above discussion teaches us that developing relationships create demands on the partners to engage in certain sorts of activity in order to 'certify' that the relationship is proceeding normally towards its expected goal point or ideal state. However, not all relationships proceed at the same rate, and individuals differ in their beliefs about the speed at which they should proceed. A study of dating couples in America (Peplau *et al.*, 1977) found that some couples who engaged in sexual intercourse within one month of meeting reported that it was due to sexual desire rather than to love, whereas those who waited for six months gave love as the 'cause' of their intercourse rather than just sexual desire. It seems very likely that some couples prefer to delay sex until they feel emotionally close, while others use sexual intercourse as a way of creating greater feelings of commitment and, as it were, make themselves fall in love as a result. The timing of first intercourse does not seem to affect a couple's perceptions of the closeness of their relationship: both 'early' and 'late' couples report satisfaction to be at about the same level. Equally, 'early sex' is not more nor less likely to lead to the break up of the couple than is 'later sex'.

Some dating couples decide to go further towards an institutionalised relationship than is created by simply engaging in sexual intercourse. They choose to enter a cohabital relationship, where they live together as if they were married, but without actually going through a marriage ceremony. National samples of the USA taken before 1977 show that between 2-5 per cent of the population is cohabiting (Newcomb, 1981). People choose to live with one another without being married for all sorts of reasons and, surprisingly, in some 25 per cent of cases never actually discuss whether to cohabit before they actually do so. In these cases it just happens, or else it 'just growed' (like Topsy) and partners had spent several nights together, found it generally agreeable, and decided to continue. In cases where the couples do discuss it beforehand, there are two key influences on the decision. First, partners are influenced by opportunity, as created by such things as the availability of suitable accommodation; the attitudes, beliefs and pressures of friends; distance away from parents or authority figures; and the attractiveness that they see their partner to have. The second influence is the major one: willingness of the two partners to take advantage of the opportunities that are available. This, naturally is the major point of discussion between partners, and the decision ultimately seems to depend on religious beliefs, previous sexual experience, and the strength of liking or commitment towards the partner. Where the partners have a low religious commitment they are more likely to cohabit, although, for reasons not yet fully clarified by research, there is an over-representation of Catholics and Jewish women among cohabiting couples (Newcomb, 1981). Cohabitors of both sexes are more experienced sexually and report a wider variety of sexual practices than do people who are not cohabiting.

Some people faced with a decision to cohabit naturally decide to do so and some do not. Investigators have been interested in what makes the decision go one way or the other; and it seems to come down largely to the way in which the partners see themselves. Cohabitors have a generally more favourable view of themselves and their personality. They see themselves as more intelligent, less controlled by social restraints, less inhibited generally, more outgoing, attractive, and appreciative of art or the aesthetic things of life. One explanation for this is that cohabitation is, relatively, a more uncertain relationship than marriage and the extra social constraints, legal obligations and contractual forces of marriage provide a structure for those who need it (Newcomb, 1981). People who are more certain that their relationship will last because of their own positive qualities are probably more willing to consider the uncertain relationship of cohabitation than are those who feel insecure about their ability to retain their partner's affections or commitment to a cohabital arrangement. As indicated at the start of this chapter, then, the decision about cohabitation is taken within the framework of the partners' expectations for the relationship, and their ability to hold it together once they take the public step of committing themselves to an unconventional arrangement.

Because cohabitation is not yet a widely accepted alternative to conventional marriage, several investigators have been interested in comparing cohabiting partners with married partners in the expectation of finding differences of life-style, or in the patterning of activities that occur in such sort of relationship (see Newcomb, 1981 for a review). The most influential study found that, contrary to expectations, both married and cohabiting women performed the majority of the household tasks. Overall, there were very few differences between the two groups, despite the fact that cohabiting women see themselves as significantly more masculine (and cohabiting men as more feminine) than married persons do. The cohabitors see themselves as more unconventional, but actually operate in a way that does not distinguish them from the traditional role patterns for husband and wife. This is explained by the investigators in the study as due to the tedious efforts for the couple in constant reassessment of their behaviour in order to see whether they are acting out the 'right' roles. They too easily find themselves, over a period of time, slipping back into traditional moulds, even though their ideals call for some other line of action.

In coping with both the conventional husband-wife and the unconventional cohabital arrangement then, the persons' intentions are not enough. Demands of the situation, pressures on time, the reactions of other people, and the very powerful constraints exercised by society at large make it rather more difficult for partners to adopt their desired mix of activities than they may have hoped. As indicated earlier, the effects of a network or surrounding social system can exert a dramatic influence on people's actions in relationships, and the only really effective way of dealing with this problem is to use this knowledge to one's own advantage by surrounding oneself with a network that holds the same values, beliefs and opinions as oneself. Thus cohabital communes are more likely to work out and stick to a non-traditional pattern of relational activities than are cohabital couples who remain in a society that retains its traditional beliefs about role-based activity.

The whole problem stems from the need for any pair to work out ways of running the new form of relationship, to create behavioural strategies and indicators that square up with their feelings for one another, and to cope with the relationship itself which takes on a kind of life of its own once it reaches a high level of involvement. Partners start by liking one another, then learn to adjust to and cope with one another, and finally have to learn to adjust to and cope with everyone else's and their own responses to the fact that they are now 'in a relationship'. In this way the pair becomes 'socially acknowledged'. Outsiders treat them as a couple rather than as two individuals: where one is invited, the other is also implicitly invited, too; one partner's friends become the other person's friends, and so on. These pressures are powerful enough when they are informal but get even stronger once the relationship gets a social seal of approval and turns into 'a marriage'.

From Love to Marriage and Beyond

I have been discussing the changes that can occur to a relationship both from the inside and from the outside once it is formed. When people fall in love, so their own and other people's behaviour towards them changes in a number of ways. So also does the partners' belief that marriage is a likely result of the courtship. Such beliefs and such inside and outside pressures or influences lead the partners through courtship in a particular way and make certain patterns of activity more probable than others. The expectations also compel the partners to face up to the business of working out their future roles, planning for marriage and afterwards, and generally fixing their eyes on some point quite distant from the present. This will involve them in a certain amount of charting of their likely route towards marriage, as well as in some formation of a timescale for carrying it out. The very latest research on courtship (Huston, *et al.*, 1981) has shown that people can be divided into four categories according to the way in which they go about effecting this transition from courtship to marriage. Whereas the early stages of dating, falling in love, and courtship have a very consistent pattern to them, the later stages separate very characteristically according to the one of the four categories that the courtship pattern falls into.

Love and Courtship

In several studies of loving couples (e.g. Rubin, 1974) it has been found that they have a very consistent pattern of non-verbal behaviour (as discussed in the earlier chapters). This, of course, helps very dramatically to communicate their feelings for one another, not only to one another but also to anyone else who sees them. The behaviour serves to signal that they are a loving couple, and the actions of sitting close together, holding hands, touching, talking intimately and so on serve a very important signalling function at these stages of the blossoming relationship. More important, however, is the fact that such behaviour is not simply the result of the feelings that the partners have for one another: it *is* the relationship. It is an essential part of the state of being in love, and the quality or quantity of the loving behaviour helps both partners — and the outside world — to

97

know that the partners are in love. Individuals who do not show it satisfactorily will create problems of embarrassment for outsiders who may not know how to treat the couple. Are they really 'a couple', or should we pretend that they are not mutually involved? More important, such individuals will cause their partner dissatisfaction, frustration and, possibly, grief. The pattern consists first of a much increased level of so-called eye contact — that is, gazing into the eyes of one's partner. As I indicated in chapter 2, this is not very surprising once we realise that the eyes are the habitual medium for transmitting messages of intimacy and liking. They are far more important than words in this respect. Lovers gaze at one another in this way nearly eight times longer than strangers do when they are not actually conversing with one another. The partners are mutually interested in one another, to the exclusion of pretty well everyone and everything else: in the words of the song, 'I only have eyes for you.'

There are some other, more unexpected effects also. One experiment (Dion and Dion, 1979) showed that loving couples have a much better memory for random words read aloud by their partner, for example! Furthermore, when their partners are put into a special piece of psychological apparatus that usually creates the illusion that a person is much smaller than they really are, loving couples don't see it that way. It is almost as if love cancels out the effects of the Hall of Mirrors and distorted reflections of one's partner are instantly corrected by the effects of love.

Once love entices the couple into a working courtship their behaviour 'bottoms out' a little, and the important fact is not so much that they spend more time together (to the exclusion of other relationships), sit closer together, touch one another more, gaze into one another's eyes, and self-disclose. The important changes concern the ways in which the partners begin to distribute their time together — the changing amounts of time that they devote to different activities as their courtship develops along one of the four tracks or trajectories that research has picked up.

From Courtship to Marriage

The four types of track towards marriage are, according to Huston *et al.* (1981),

(i) *'Accelerated-arrested'*, which starts off very fast, with partners planning marriage within two or three months of meeting, but then not actually carrying out the plan for a year or so after that;

(ii) *'Accelerated'*, which leads to plans of marriage within about five months of meeting and execution of the plan within another five months or so;

(iii) *'Intermediate'*, where the partners do not plan marriage for certain until about a year or so, and then marry within about eight months of that; and

(iv) *'Prolonged'*, where the couple take a relatively retarded and rocky path to marriage.

The last two types of courtship show the greatest problems, with more conflicts and turbulence than the first two types of courtship, despite the fact that they have longest to practise the behaviour that will be required in their eventual marriage.

In all types of courtship there are some common patterns of activity that characterise the growth of the relationship (Huston, *et al.*, 1981). For example, although partners spend an increasing proportion of their available time with each other rather than with their other friends, the time is not spent just in the affectionate activities that sustain the relationship so much as in the practical tasks of living. Daily tasks are done together more often than one might expect. It is predictable, on the other hand, that partners would spend more time in leisure activities together. It is found in all the types of courtship that they do this to the exclusion of leisure activities with other people. In short, the individuals withdraw from their relationships with other people and draw towards their partner more exclusively.

There are, however, key differences between the courtship types also. 'Intermediate' courtships show the lowest levels of commitment to one another. The partners show less affection, do not work together so much on tasks, and spend more time alone than persons in other courtship types do, including those in the very longest 'prolonged' courtships. By contrast, the partners in both sorts of 'accelerated' courtship report greater closeness and affection, and they work together more closely on tasks, particularly those that are traditionally associated with the female role.

Researchers find that the activities that accompany the growth of a courtship towards marriage are not the same for all couples (Huston, *et al.*, 1981). The shortest courtships do not necessarily report more love at the early stages, but the couples do work out faster and better the way in which to work together in the relationship. They cope more rapidly with the problems and everyday tasks that benefit from the co-operative input of both partners, such as joint decision-making and household tasks. By contrast, the long courtships seem to be more full of love and affection: the partners just have greater difficulty getting agreement on how the tasks of life should be performed and by whom. Accordingly, these slowly progressing courtships require the partners to put much more of their time and effort into just maintaining and sustaining the relationship (see next section). This probably slows them down by diverting them from the real job in courtship — negotiating and working out how the future marriage will actually be performed. Complex relationships like marriage involve not only the mutual affection and commitment of both partners, but also their ability to mesh their behaviour together satisfactorily in matters like housekeeping, providing and decision-making. They have to negotiate who will be responsible for which parts of the domestic tasks of marriage, and to work out satisfactory ways of acting out the roles of husband and wife. Marital stability depends not merely on affection but on the ability to co-ordinate efforts on such tasks. The roles of husband and wife are complementary: they mesh together, although there is no generally ideal way of doing this, and each pair of partners must negotiate their own solution to the problem during courtship and beyond.

Marital problems are strongly associated with a poor fit between the partners' expectations and beliefs about their respective marital roles (Newcomb and Bentler, 1981). Where partners have a great deal of specialisation and demarcation of the household duties and in the types of decisions that each partner takes, then marital happiness is generally low. On the contrary, marriages with egalitarian roles are usually better ad-justed than those where either partner is excessively dominant and controlling. So, once again, the research indicates that those partners who successfully work out an agreeable way to distribute their activities will generate a more satisfactory relationship. Such activities cannot be left to chance and do not simply fall into place if a couple is deeply in love. The activities *are* the relationship, and require the work, time, effort, attention and skill of the partners. It is important that couples who intend to marry give thought to such things, and talk carefully over their beliefs about the marital roles, about the distribution of labour, and about the pattern of activities even if they are deeply in love. The feelings alone will not make the marriage as happy as will the satisfactory creation of complementary roles and ways of behaving in marriage. The couple who are constantly yelling at one another may start to do so through anger, but gradually come to 'fix' in the pattern because they see themselves doing it: obviously, they begin to think, if we shout at one another like that we can't like one another very much! They perceive themselves to be acting in a way that is inconsistent with close feelings, so they explain their behaviour as caused by dislike. This is exactly the opposite explanation from the one we are used to: we usually think of feelings causing behaviour, but in some cases behaviour causes feelings.

It is thus very important for couples to spend time negotiating and setting up patterns of activity and complementary roles of behaving that would help them to feel that they are close. For men, at least, the rewards of doing so are very significant, even vital in the literal sense. Happily married men have superior mental health, lower suicide rates, greater career prospects and longer lives (Bloom *et al.*, 1978). Small wonder that the most farsighted business organisations are keenly interested in the stability of their executives' marriages. Happily married executives stay healthier and actually do a better job! For women, the picture is not quite so rosy as is indicated by the fact that women are responsible for the legal initiation of about 75 per cent of all divorces (Hagestad and Smyer, 1982). Equally, most recent research shows that the part of the population most depressed is composed of non-working married women with pre-school age children — just those people most often represented by the media as most fulfilled. It seems, however, that women are better at coping with intimacy, partly because they

rarely concentrate all their intimacy needs into one relationship. They usually have a wide range of friends who are not (as
men's friends often are) simply concentrated around the workplace. For this reason women are possibly better at developing
intimacy through the activities and behaviour I have been
describing, since they have a wider and broader range of
experience to draw on. It is certainly the women who handle the
development of courtship better and actually take more of the
management role. But as with so many other things, it may be
the happily married men who end up getting the greater
benefits from this.

From 'Married Couple' to 'Family'

A major change that takes place in the activities of a married
couple is brought about by the addition of children. What has
been said already in this book will prepare us to expect that the
change in activities can cause feelings to change also, and will
affect the couple's satisfaction with their marriage, with their
partner, and with themselves. Particularly for the wife, a
consistent finding in several studies over many years is that
satisfaction with the marriage very often declines very sharply
just after children are born (Newcomb and Bentler, 1981). The
wife's satisfaction with herself is also affected. While these
findings are very consistent, some couples emerge from the
trough much more successfully than others, and it is becoming
clear that it is those couples who create the best patterns of
activity that cope best. The birth of children affects the way in
which a couple can distribute their time, and also affects the
tasks they do together. As I have shown, this affects their view of
the relationship: since they spend less time alone and spend
more time doing tasks related to the child, so they come to see
themselves as less caring for one another, unless they take the
trouble to create and negotiate a more satisfying view of what
they are doing. This can be done by the obvious means of
forcing more time alone together into their daily timetable; but
this is not always possible, and 'special treat outings' can merely
throw into sharp relief the fact that they are special, unusual
and rare. A less obvious, but ultimately more successful, way of
coping with the problem is to reconstrue the tasks as 'relationship activity', that is, to grow from seeing them merely as jobs to

be done, and to come to see them as indications of the strength of relationship, opportunities for sharing, examples of emotional commitment to the marriage and the family, and so on. This relatively subtle psychological shift pulls the activity back into the relationship domain, rather than leaving partners to feel as if it is work done at the expense of the relationship. It is thus a way of preserving the couple's feelings for each other and, incidentally, of strengthening their mutual bond to the child. Accordingly, it creates a smoother transition from marriage to family — a transition that is not simply the result of the birth of the child, but of the negotiation of a newly-organised relationship. A family is a relationship that is a psychological creation much more than it is simply a numerical one.

This fact is further illustrated by the relational change that comes later as the children grow. Because the parents are the major agents who turn the child into a social being and help to create its sociable tendencies, skills and understandings, they are very often in conflict with the child's unsociable, selfish, even animal nature. They spend time dealing with the children's conflicts between themselves, with school problems, and with disagreements between parent and child over discipline. Those families that pay close attention to this problem as a relationship problem rather than as a discipline problem will be the ones that cope better and adjust to it more successfully. It is necessary to put in hard work to focus themselves away from these issues as routine discipline tasks, and onto them as relationship matters or onto other activities that bring about more positive attitudes to the relationship between parent and child.

According to the most influential studies discussed in Burgess (1981), parents can establish one of three sorts of relationship with their children. They can be *authoritarian*, that is, they can try to control and relate to their child by stressing the value of obedience, and will use punishment to enforce it. They can be *permissive*, that is, they exert little control over the child, consult the child about standards of behaviour, and use reason rather than punishment to exercise their child-rearing duties. Both of these types of relationship lead, in their own different ways, to disaster. The former produces over-anxious children who are dependent and unduly cowed by authority, rules and social pressures. The second leads to self-indulgent children who show little respect for other people. In short, the relationship that the child experiences itself will affect the range and style of relationship that it is capable of forming with other people later in life. The key piece in the jigsaw is the way in which the child learns through its relationship with its parents to perceive itself.

A third style of parental relationship with the child, *authoritative*, has been shown to be the most successful in respect of its immediate task of inducing proper suitable behaviour and also in respect of the long-term goal of helping the child develop into an adult capable of establishing good relationships with other adults. In the authoritiative parental style, the parent relies on reason and consistency rather than taking each instance as it comes. The child is not consulted, as by permissive parents, but is given firm guidance on the principles that are being used in a given case to exercise control. The general style is caring and supportive rather than indulgent, and this generally promotes a high self-esteem along with good reasoning ability, responsibility and independence in relationships with other people.

As with all other relationships, the good and the bad relationships of parents with children have characteristically different patterns of activity and of communication. Poor parental relationships with children are characterised by an accent on the negative; that is, they tend to focus on failure, to be critical and punitive, and to ignore or underplay the child's successes. A second feature of such relationships is that the parents are very poor observers of the child's behaviour: they do not notice or attend to differences in the child's activities from day to day, do not recognise such differences as 'failure through not trying' and 'failure despite trying hard'. Consequently they tend to be inconsistent in their use of punishment; in particular they issue very many threats and scolds, but do not carry them out. Most important of all, poor parental relationships with children are those where parents are very rarely warm or positive about the children or the children's efforts (Burgess, 1981). This tends to create low self-esteem in the children and to make it difficult for people to motivate them to do things, except by coercion and threat. They are used to being driven from behind by stick and strap, rather than encouraged from the front by carrot and reward.

As with the kinds of relationships discussed earlier, the

research makes it clear that marital and family satisfaction depend not only on achievement of satisfactory patterns of activity but also on careful attention to communication. Happily married couples talk to each other more, convey the clear impression that they understand the other person, show more sensitivity to their partner's feelings, and supplement their speech with a more expressive range of non-verbal signals. In short, they adopt a pattern of communication that conveys understanding and a willingness to open out about their own feelings. Comparable findings sharply contrast distressed and happy families: distressed families have not skilfully created a pattern of communication that stresses interest in the other people's views, sentiments and beliefs. Instead, they are low on the humourous banter and strong emotional support that characterises the normal and most successful happy families.

The Empty Nest

Clearly, a major change in a family's structure and general styles of activity will follow when the children grow up and leave home (Dickens and Perlman, 1981). Not only do the parental couple lose the amount of contact that they are used to having with their child, but they have to cope with other incidental consequences. For example, contact with neighbours decreases, particularly with relatively distant neighbours. This seems to be due to the fact that the children and the children's friends serve an important function in linking neighbours together. People who would not normally meet are brought together by the common tasks of child-rearing and the common concerns that parents have about discipline, education and employment. Once the children remove this social lynch pin, the neighbourly relationships fall apart.

This effect on relationship patterns is compensated for many people by a sharp increase in their involvement with club and social activities in middle age. In the years leading up to retirement, people often go through a period of marked expansion of their social activity before retirement, while old age brings about a steady reduction in such activity. It may be partly in preparation for retirement and in response to a feeling of still having much left to give to other people, and partly as a response to the loneliness brought about by the reduction in social activity once children leave home. Since children obviously satisfy many of the friendship needs that parents have, their absence makes the need more acute and the parents set about satisfying them in other relationships. They do this by undertaking different sorts of interests, tasks and activities.

Another major adjustment that the couple must make to the empty nest is getting used to being alone together once again, and to having only themselves for company in the home (Reisman, 1981; Chown, 1981). This adjustment is another example of all the points made earlier. It is an adjustment to changes in the patterns of behaviour and of communication, rather than to feelings about one another. Yet changes in their feelings are often a direct consequence, and those couples who adjust by spending more of their time as relationship time rather than task time or, worse, wasted time, will be most successful in effecting the adaptations. As with all of the other examples given in this chapter, such adaptive adjustments are important ways of changing relationships, or of coping with change. However, they are also fundamental to the maintenance and sustenance of satisfying relationships, to which I now turn.

Maintaining Satisfying Relationships

In the earlier sections in this chapter and in the previous chapter I have focused on the ways in which a relationship grows, and on the ways in which growth and change have to be shown and represented through the actions of the partners. This is a very important feature of the creation of any relationship, for if it does not develop the relationship will probably perish. However, once any relationship has reached a level of intimacy that satisfies the two partners, they have to maintain it at that level, keep it in trim, and work to ensure that it stays satisfactory for them both. Many relationships perish through the fact that the partners are careless in maintaining it or nourishing it once it has grown to fullness.

In any discussion of maintenance of relationships, it is particularly difficult to specify the behaviours that are necessary in order to keep the relationship going. The range of relevant circumstances in each different type of relationship is simply too vast for this to be possible. Instead, research has identified a strategy, an approach, an orientation or a style that is most effective (Walster *et al.*, 1978). Essentially, it is based on 'fairness' rather than on the benefits or rewards that a particular person gets out of the relationship. In maintaining relationships, people have a very strong preference for things to be fair, rather than wanting to exploit and get out of them all that they can. When a relationship is not fair for both partners, it hits the rocks extremely hard and the partners employ various correction devices that this section will describe.

Investigators have found a resistance on some people's part to thinking of close relationships in terms of fairness, because of a feeling that it is not possible to measure what happens in intimate contexts (Hatfield and Traupmann, 1981). If no measurements can be taken, then it is not possible to evaluate whether everything is balanced, fair and even. However, many people feel that they are able to measure something about their relationships: they can, for instance, form some idea of whether their partner seems to love them as much as they love their partner. People can also tell when they are being let down, poorly treated, ignored, over-indulged, allowed to get away with blue murder, and so on. These vague feelings are all imprecise ways of evaluating the relationship, and the fact that we have the words to describe such evaluations tells us something about the fact that the feelings are very real for the people involved, even if they are not mathematically precise or scientifically valid. People feel as if they can measure fairness in a relationship, and what truly counts to them is precisely the fact that they do or do not feel that they are getting a fair deal. So we should look at fairness in terms of what people think they and their partner are getting out of the relationship. Successful relationships will be sustained when each person ensures that his or her partner feels fairly treated.

We have already come across the idea that the type of relationship and its success are partly defined by the resources that are exchanged in it: by what the partners do for one another, whether they do it for love or money, out of duty, or because they have been promised some attractive service in return. Examples of resources were given earlier as compliments, gifts, advice, services, money, help, and so on. We have also

107

considered the idea that exchanges have usually to be balanced out if they are to survive, but that as the relationship develops and gets closer, so people extend their timespan. They don't expect to receive an exactly equivalent reward immediately in exchange for one that they give. Instead, as the relationship grows, they are more and more prepared to accept longer delays for exchange, different types of 'repayment' and so on. Whereas beginning acquaintances are very attentive to reciprocity, and expect equal repayment fairly soon, this desire diminishes the stronger the relationship gets (Hatfield and Traupmann, 1981). Indeed, one sign that the relationship is growing well is when the partners notice that they don't feel pressured or obliged to reciprocate every reward, or every disclosure that their partner gives.

Whilst this is increasingly true in developing relationships, people still do have a notion of fairness in the long term. We all know that we give up on relationships where we have to do all the work to keep them going, or where friends rarely help us, but expect help whenever they themselves need it, and so on. Yet in long-term relationships we are also prepared to extend a kind of social 'hire purchase' facility, and to do things for friends, spouses or family that we would expect to be repaid at any time in the distant future, or by some other means than exact reciprocity.

Nevertheless, once the fairness of a relationship starts to feel out of balance the partners soon revert to focusing on the exchange more closely, and most lovers' tiffs or friends' quarrels are caused by their feeling that the balance is extremely un-evenly set. Homely examples of such occurrences are provided by statements like 'I've been doing all this housework for weeks now and you haven't taken me out once', and 'I've been slaving away at work to earn enough to take you on holiday and I deserve a rest at home.'

After much debate, researchers like Walster *et al.* (1978) have decided that although there are many sorts of fairness, there is only one that really counts in maintaining relationships satisfactorily: equity. Equity is a particular sort of fairness, as the following example makes clear. If I have £200 to share out fairly between four people who worked on a job, I could give everyone the same amount. Researchers call this *parity*. Or I could give the most to the person with the greatest need for the money, and least to the one who was already well-off. Researchers refer to this as *Marxist justice*. Or I could give the most to the person who worked the hardest and least to the person who did the least. This is *equity*, and researchers have assumed that people will be happy with their relationships when they feel that their rewards are equitable with their efforts. If they have to put up with a lot in a relationship (e.g. if they have a friend who has very severe changes in mood, a quick temper and is often irritable) then the amount of love, help, advice or entertainment that they receive from the partner will also have to be a lot.

Because there are two people in a relationship, there is an extra factor to take into account in working out what is equitable: namely, what the general outcome received from the relationship by the partner is and how it matches up to the person's own outcomes. If a person feels that his partner is getting exactly the same outcome and rewards from the relationship, but is doing less or putting up with less in order to get them, then the person will feel that the relationship is inequitable, even if the rewards are exactly the same. Equally, even if I have to put in an awful lot of effort for very small reward (e.g. nursing a sick friend) I may nevertheless feel that the relationship is equitable because the friend has to suffer so much more to receive the perhaps slightly greater rewards. In this case our rewards may not be equal, but neither are the costs and efforts, and we shall both still feel that the relationship is an equitable one that we wish to preserve.

It should be clear that both the costs and the rewards in relationships can be either psychological or physical. Psychological costs might be things like humiliation and insult; examples of physical ones would be effort and loss of money. Psychological rewards could be compliments, love and respect; and physical ones may be help in mending a car, or a gift of a book. In considering the equity or inequity of friendships, people will consider both psychological and physical rewards and costs. They can decide that their relationship is equitable, or that they are over-benefited (i.e. receive more than they should) or under-benefited (i.e. receive less than they should).

Just as the rewards and costs can be psychological or actual ones, so can people's responses to inequity (Hatfield and Traupmann, 1981). That is, someone may decide to respond to inequity either by actually doing something about it, or by adjusting their psychological attitude to it. For instance, in the last two cases they will be unhappy (guilty when they are over-benefited, angry when under-benefited) and will try to do something about it, either by leaving the relationship, or by altering their opinion or evaluation of it. ('I have to put up with a lot, but where am I going to find someone who knows so much about my pet love: Czechoslovak medieval history?')

We are probably used to hearing about under-benefit as a cause of bad feelings about a relationship and consequent unhappiness with maintaining it, but over-benefit can have the same negative effects (Walster *et al.*, 1978). For example, where people are showered with goods and attention beyond the capacity to respond, or far beyond what they feel they reasonably deserve, then they may feel so guilty or so uneasy and awkward that they want to withdraw from the relationship either physically (e.g. by leaving) or psychologically (e.g. by treating the other person extremely casually and patronisingly, as if they didn't really care). So generosity and kindess can actually make people want to leave a friendship rather than stay in it, and pairs of friends or marital partners need to achieve equity rather than excessive loving and kindness by one partner alone.

Difficulties, problems or ineptness in conducting relationships equitably can thus lead to the disruption or even the dissolution of the relationship. The practical implications of this are that individuals need to assess the equity of their relationships from time to time, whilst still recognising that strict equality of exchange is the mark of a beginning relationship rather than a fully-fledged and well-developed one. Since equity means taking account of one's partner's outcomes as well as one's own, this is naturally a good practice anyway since it involves focusing on the general state of the relationship rather than just on one's own wishes, desires, rewards and efforts. In maintaining any of the relationships that I have considered in the present chapter, equity is an important factor, therefore. However, there are several other features of maintaining relationships, and these must also be handled with tact and skill — particularly conflict, arguments and tensions.

Conflicts and tensions naturally arise in every sort of relationship from time to time, but recent research suggests that, far from being the destructive force that most of us would predict, conflict can actually help maintain or even develop a relationship if it is managed right. Presumably a conflict that can be resolved actually focuses the two partners on the instability of their relationship, but also upon the benefit that would be lost if the relationship were to die (Braiker and Kelley, 1979). Resolution of the conflict reaffirms the partners' faith in each other, as well as stressing that they have chosen to avoid the consequences of breaking up. Interestingly, conflict has been shown to increase quite sharply from the period of 'casual dating' to the establishment of the relationship as 'serious dating'. From then on it levels off, but it is interesting that conflict is growing at the very time when the relationship is growing too.

The factors that determine whether or not a conflict will be disruptive or constructive seem to be relatively obvious ones like the manner in which it is conducted, and its content or what it is about, as well as the style of the discussions that surround it. Yet a tendency to avoid conflict can be equally destructive if it prevents a couple from dealing with the issue that causes the concern. Effective ways of coping with conflict have been found to be strategies like openly communicating about the distress that is felt, as well as about the cause itself, and explaining carefully to the partner at each step the consequences that particular actions have had for one's own feelings (Kaplan, 1976). Willingness to disclose one's feelings is very strongly related to successful marriage and, conversely, there is much more likely to be disruption in a marriage where there is very little mutual sharing of feelings. The same is true of organisational conflict between managers and personnel, between teachers and pupils, and between colleagues at work. Open but controlled expression of feelings about a source of conflict makes it possible for partners to treat the task of healing the rift as a personal, relationship-oriented task whilst also allowing each person to rid himself of pent-up resentments. More important, it prevents them from adopting the covert type of conflict that means openly avoiding discussion of some key problem ('ostrich activity') or simply acting as if it does not exist and cannot be discussed ('repressive handling'). The worst form, however, is the 'empty relationship' style where partners speak in an exaggeratedly affectionate way, but deliberately act in ways that show contempt, disdain or irritation. This latter style has been found to characterise older married couples, who presumably see little alternative if they are beyond the age where they could have a reasonable expectation of finding a substitute for their present partner (Hagestad and Smyer, 1982). In such cases the couple are acting under the pressure of social constraints that keep them together, rather than under the pressure of desire for one another. The barriers to dissolution of the relationship are habit, social pressure from neighbours and friends, fear of the consequences of leaving, and so on. As we shall see in chapter 6, the way of repairing and correcting such relationships is markedly different from the repairing techniques suitable with loving couples who are finding the relationship hard to fulfil, or with children who are unpopular. In order to get a proper run at the issues of breakdown and repair of relationships, I shall consider children's friendships in the next chapter, since childhoods lays the foundations not only for good relationships but also for bad ones.

Summary

In dealing with prolonged intimate relationships I have concentrated on the changes in patterns of activity that characterise major changes in the intimacy of a relationship, and I have again stressed the absolute importance of such changes. Relationships do not grow at all if the partners do not change the activities that they perform together. This chapter has considered the shaping force of expectations about a relationship and other social or surrounding pressures. All of these beliefs, pressures and forces influence changes in the relationship such as engaging in sexual intercourse, and deciding to marry or cohabit. Similar kinds of change in activity are necessary when courting or married couples negotiate their respective roles of 'wife' and 'husband'. This negotiation means they work to create a system of complementary activity. Further changes follow when there is an addition of children to the family and the changing pattern of activities requires careful attention and adjustment if the relationship is to survive undisturbed — or even if the partners are to stay in love with one another. Relationships need not only to be developed but also maintained, and the chapter considered the influences and processes that establish fairness in the relationship as a key principle of satisfaction. At this later stage of relationships liking alone is not enough to sustain a relationship: partners have to develop good ways of acting together and helping to create the machinery of the relationship.

5

Roots: Children's Friendships

In the previous chapters I have been stressing that satisfying adult relationships have to be created through behaviour, and that this requires many different skills and abilities. Whilst I have also noted the differences between people's capacities to carry out the necessary skills, I have not yet considered where these differences may arise. The answer, of course, is that they originate in childhood, where the foundations of all adult relationships are laid. Childhood and adolescence are the places and times where the various skills are first acquired, practised and developed. Each skill has to be picked up and polished, not only as an essential ingredient of later friendship abilities but also at a time that is right and useful for the child's conduct of its own relationships with its contemporaries. There are thus two problems for the child: first, learning to relate in a way acceptable to its peers or contemporaries at the time; second, learning the skills of friendship that will be a good grounding for relationships in later life.

Childhood relationships are, of course, important throughout the whole time of childhood, and they can exert strong influences on the development of character and personality, as is well known. It is perhaps less well known that they have been shown to affect educational achievement, and there are some researchers who believe that intelligence itself can be affected (see Asher and Gottman, 1981). The relationships in childhood can affect a child's understanding of complex problems and influence the development of its comprehension of relationships between objects, between concepts, and between people, as well as having a predictable effect on the child's happiness. For example, unpopular children perform poorly at school, experience learning difficulties, and drop out of school in much greater numbers than their popular peers (see Putallaz and Gottman, 1981). However, the most significant aspect of relationships in childhood is the fact that the clearly shape adult relationships in childhood is the fact that they clearly shape adult them. In childhood, some children experience such difficulties with relationships, or are so unpopular, that the consequent resentment makes them generally hostile and resistant to intimacy, or else hopelessly dependent and over-sensitive. These effects can be very far-reaching and are only just being fully realised. Unpopular children are more likely to become juvenile delinquents, to be disgracefully discharged from the armed services, to have higher rates of emotional and mental health problems in adulthood, and to be at higher risk of schizophrenia, neurosis and psychosis (see Putallaz and Gottman, 1981). It is also quite clear from the depressingly small amounts of research work that are funded to investigate children's friendships that the socially withdrawn, socially incompetent and aggressive child soon becomes the socially inept adult social casualty. For example, the most famous mass murderers of almost every country (e.g. Christie, the Black Panther, Blue Beard, the Michigan Murderer, the Boston Strangler, and others) have invariably been found to have had abnormal social experiences in childhood, or to have ben left without adult help or guidance when they ran into difficulties with their peers — whether the people in the same school classes, same age cohort, or same playgroups. They are usually found to have been loners, quiet types and unsociable people, often dominated by selfish parents, or hounded by thoughtless classmates. If friendmaking had been properly learned — or if they had been helped to learn — their violent, destructive and unusual personalities may have turned out in a more rewarding and acceptable form. However, the large number of people whose personalities go wrong in only minor ways from the same cause are much more important and significant than these extreme cases, and I shall spend the rest of the chapter with them in mind.

The full extent of this problem has not previously been fully appreciated because the consequences of poor relations in childhood are hidden, and only just beginning to come clearly and obviously into the light. Even problems like truancy and delinquency are still often viewed as problems in their own right rather than as possible consequences of inability to form proper friendships at school. Yet research in prisons for the especially dangerous and the criminally insane has shown that many violent offenders have developed peculiar and abnormal ideas about friendship, often showing attitudes that are characteristic of retarded or arrested social and relational development (Howells, 1981). Moreover, British and American work on alcoholics casts up time and time again cases of adults who turned to excessive drinking because their relationships are not satisfactory, and as children they had not learned to put them right (Orford and O'Reilly, 1981).

It is necessary at the outset, therefore, to stress that there exist many forms of the bad results of poor childhood relationships. Unpopularity can follow such oddities as an uncommon first name, unattractive physical appearance or atypical racial origin; while factors such as classroom size, organisation of desks, cloakrooms, teaching materials and the personality of the teacher can also be influential (Putallaz and Gottman, 1981). Nevertheless, by far and away the most important influence is the faulty learning that the child does about friendship.

Learning to make friends — and how to make friends — is something that everyone has to do in the early years in the family, at play, and at school (Foot *et al.*, 1980). Friendmaking ability is absolutely not instinctive nor genetically programmed; nor is it something that is inherited; rather, it is something that comes about through, and in the social experiences of, childhood and adolescence. It is something that has to be acquired, learned carefully, and practised. This raises the interesting question of why it is all treated so casually. We all believe that it is absurd to expect children and adolescents to develop academic or intellectual knowledge without help and guidance, but we just seem to expect them to develop satisfactory social abilities on their own. Despite the fact that it is one of the most important, far-reaching and continuous lessons of children's lives, it is at present a lesson learned through chance alone, due to appalling neglect of this basic social fact It is at present a lesson, therefore, where accident and coincidence have a persistent, uncorrected influence and where they can turn and twist a personality forever. It is a lesson that some people learn well, some grasp with difficulty but with eventual success, and some learn so poorly that it afflicts their adult relationship with a social canker. Yet it remains true that with equal consistency governments and educators ignore the research, and are quite happy to allow the seeds of a whole field of later social problems to be fed and watered by inadequate or threatening playground experiences.

The problems result from faulty learning of many different sorts of friendship skills (Foot *et al.*, 1980; Rubin, 1980; La Gaipa, 1981). The natural growth and development that take place in childhood give children new capacities for learning, and also place new problems in their way. As they develop in other ways, therefore, so must they develop new and additional friendship skills. Friendship involves, as we have seen, a reasonable level of self-esteem, an understanding of the meaning of co-operation, ability to use and comprehend non-verbal behaviour, recognition of the activities that suit a particular level and style of relationship, trust, intimacy, self-disclosure, and an ability to reciprocate — and that is an incomplete list. To some extent children pick these items up separately, practise them, consolidate them, and go on to the next one. Failure to pick up one element may create problems in moving on to the next one, or may 'throw' the whole process of learning.

What then *do* children need to learn from and about friendship at different ages? How does it shape their view of themselves, their comprehension of life, and their future relationships? In addressing such questions I shall pay particular attention to the research that has identified effective training or correctional strategies for cases where things are going wrong.

The Child's Friendship World

Childhood actually covers a considerable span of years, and much that can be said of its beginning will not still be true of its ending in adolescence. Friendship is a clear example here, since many aspects of it change during childhood, both in terms of how the child thinks about friendship at different ages, and in terms of how children behave with and to their friends as they grow more mature. However one item which is consistently being shaped and moulded in early childhood is the child's view

117

of himself (self-image) and the child's belief about his value or acceptability to other people (self-acceptance). It has often been noted by psychiatric theorists that people who cannot accept themselves cannot accept others, in other words, people with a poor self-image or low self-acceptance will tend to be hostile or rejecting towards other people (Duck, 1977). They are nervous of entering close relationships in adulthood, and are mercurially unstable or unpredictable when they feel that they are becoming vulnerable; for example, when their relationships become intimate they may become irrationally agitated and even violent. Such people find adult relationships difficult, unpredictable and explosive. Since they cannot handle them easily, they also find it hard to enter or sustain friendships, or they start them off well enough but react wildly and oddly when 'cornered' into intimacy. Most normal, but untrained, outsiders will not understand why such a person acts this way, and will not be able to give the encouragement that is needed — which makes matters worse.

It seems clear that the parent who devotes energy to creating in the very young child a favourable self-image is doing that child at least as much good as a parent who devotes time to teaching the child to read at an early age. There are, after all, several types of social advantage: good education is only one of them; good social relationships are the other. For this reason a wise parent will draw the child's attention to its competences, growths of learning, increasing capacities and its skills in a way that makes it aware of its ability to cope in a variety of situations. Such assistance need not be uncritical, but should stress the successes more than the failures and will give advice, guidance and the rewards of attention once the child attempts new or difficult tasks, whether these be physical, intellectual or social. Encouraging the child to notice its successful interactions with adults and with other children is a useful way of protecting and improving its self-image, thus increasing self-esteem.

While the child's sense of self-acceptance most probably originates in the very first years of interacting with parents, there is considerable scientific controversy over the question of whether such effects can be reversed or undone (La Gaipa, 1981). Once the child goes to school, for instance, it encounters a whole new range of people and new situations which it could find so different from home that it shows a completely different range of responses — perhaps more confident ones. On the other hand, however, it has become clear from some of the most recent research that it is necessary for children to learn some basic social skills before they go to school where they have to meet and befriend other children on their own initiative rather that at their parents' prompting (Kafer, 1981). If for some reason, such as low self-esteem, the child has not yet learned the appropriate skills for friendly behaviour with other children, then school probably just exposes the child to a wider range of social learning experiences that end in failure. A lot depends on how the child responds to the inevitable rejections that all children receive. Children with high self-esteem are better prepared to let rejection just 'wash over' them, and try again. Others with low self-esteem tend to withdraw, make fewer and fewer attempts to initiate other friendships, and so become isolated. On the other hand, another ineffective strategy is to become noisy, rebellious, boastful and, ultimately, a nuisance to teachers and classmates: this attempt to attract notice also leads to isolation. The first unsuccessful strategy for dealing with rejection, then, leads to hesitancy in starting off friendships and to lack of interest in gaining acceptance by other children. The second is simply an incompetent way of attempting to gain acceptance. In their own way each of them protects the child from further problems of rejection. Kafer's (1981) research shows that the first kind of strategy protects the child from encountering rejection: it simply enables the child to avoid rejection because it avoids both the situations where rejection can be expressed, and the people who will express it. The second strategy is more subtly based. Investigators believe that the incompetent attention-seekers are actually less perceptive, and that they constantly misinterpret other people's behaviour so that they do not see rejection as rejection. It is as if they come to live in a fantasy world where they misperceive a slap in the face as a very subtle kind of welcome! This is less painful for them than it would be to recognise that they are truly being rejected.

Such defensive strategies are complex ways for the child to protect itself from having to recognise that it is really disliked. They are psychological defences against a feeling of inadequacy (Kafer, 1981). In some very sophisticated way, the defences help

119

the child to compensate for the fact that it fears dislike and rejection, or feels inadequate in social settings. The child therefore protects and defends itself by coming to avoid situations that would confirm its inadequacy, or else by coming to misperceive such confirmation when it occurs. The root cause of both of these strategic twists of psychological development lies in self-esteem. A child who acquires a low self-esteem and low self-acceptance will be an incompetent relater, will be poor and inadequate in its relationships with other people, and will need to develop such defensive strategies for coping with rejection.

Whilst the child's self-esteem level is set on track very early, and perhaps responds predominantly to the influence of parents and family, much of its other detailed learning about social relationships is derived from social experiences with friends, peers or other children. It is, after all, such people that the child spends most time with throughout the decade-and-a-half of growing maturity, and it is a peer who will eventually become its marriage partner. If the early relationships with parents sour or spoil the basis on which such relationships will be formed, considerable efforts may be necessary to correct the child's behaviour in play with other young children. However, its behaviour reflects its internal beliefs: people behave in particular ways because they believe that it is an effective or appropriate way to act or one that serves some deep or unconscious purpose. If the beliefs are wrong or twisted by reactions to some horrible experiences, then the behaviour will be wrong or twisted in consequence. Accordingly, the proper place to direct corrective energy is towards the beliefs that make the child do what it does; towards the expectations that it has about friendship; towards the concepts and notions that it has concerning co-operation and friendliness. A useful addition to such work is the coaching of disturbed or incompetent children in the other behavioural skills of friendship. I shall look at these ideas in turn.

When children begin to play with one another they are usually under the supervision of an adult, and their activities are to a very large extent restricted, constrained and determined by that fact. Once they get old enough to be independent initiators of play (when they can independently form and carry out desires to go round and play with neighbours' children, for example) their actions in friendship also change. Of course, their desires for friendship and social contact will be shaped to a very large extent by their level of self-esteem, but assuming that they do seek friendship then their behaviour and beliefs change in characteristic ways. Very young children are not naturally social and, as parents of toddlers (say of eighteen months) will know, two such children do not so much play *with* one another as play in each other's presence. They do not co-operate; they do not share things; they do not act together, or play jointly. However, they do prefer to be with another child rather than be left alone, and gradually they come to act co-operatively, to acknowledge each other, and to enter into the wonderful world of joint fantasy and shared imagination that 4-year-olds can enjoy. As far as a child in the first stages of development is concerned, if they desire friendships with other children and are capable of creating them, friends are defined by their proximity (La Gaipa, 1981). That is, a friend is someone who lives nearby or who is met fairly frequently. A friend is a momentary playmate, and is valued for its possessions, toys or physical characteristics and is assumed to think in exactly the same way as the child itself, or to enjoy exactly the same activities. At a later stage (from about four years) children get better at differ- entiating their own viewpoint from that of their friend, but they do not yet recognise the necessity of give-and-take in relation- ships (La Gaipa, 1981). The friend is valued and appreciated for what he or she can do for the individual. It is not until about the age of six that the child begins to understand that co-operation, reciprocity or 'turn-and-turn-about' is important for friend- ship. Nevertheless, they still see their own self-interest as being most important in the friendship, and are not truly or genuinely concerned about mutual interests or the friend's needs. From about the age of nine the child begins to shift towards a more objective and less self-centred view (La Gaipa, 1981). Friend- ship is seen as collaboration with other people in the furtherance of mutual common goals or interests. However, the research also shows that children of this age regard friendship as a possessive and exclusive relationship, which means that a 'best friend' cannot really have other friendships too, and still remain a best friend. The final stage of recognising the friend's autonomy and rights to other relationships does not truly come until about the age of twelve (La Gaipa, 1981). A 12-year-old comes to respect the fact that one person cannot fulfil all of his personal and psychological needs in one exclusive relationship and that independence is not only acceptable but desirable.

Thus the child's understanding of the purposes of friendship is one aspect of it that develops dramatically and changes fundamentally during the growth toward maturity. One thing that the research makes clear is that essential learning about friendship concepts can be as haphazard as it is far-reaching in its personal significance to the child (Asher and Gottman, 1981; Foot *et al.*, 1980). Just as there are children who are intellectually advantaged in any schoolroom, so there are some who are relatively advanced in their understanding of friendship — and equally, some who would benefit from greater attention and help with the social learning that they need to complete. As yet, this important feature of their development is left in the lap of the playground gods, despite the fact that these abilities to understand will affect the child's friendships and social behaviour in ways corresponding to the other intellectual changes and developments that occur. The point here is that the child's understanding of social action changes and develops from one where other children are simply responsive objects in their social world, to being one where joint activity can be enjoyed. At early ages an interest in joint activities permits children to explore the world more effectively. Such activities also start to give children someone to measure themselves against, and with whom to form impressions of the limits of their own abilities and capacities: that is, they help to develop further and clarify the detail of their level of self-esteem, whether high or low. There is not much point in parents' trying to encourage very young toddlers to be sociable: they simply don't properly understand what is meant by 'sharing' and 'playing *with* John'. However, placing them in situations where they have access to other children can increase their social potential, although not by much. The early stages are ones where self-esteem is a better focus of parental attention. In other respects the growth of understanding cannot be forced, and nature has to be allowed to run its course, while the child develops its conception of the meaning of friendship. Such development largely parallels its development in other conceptual areas, like problem solving and reasoning.

This is not to say that even at nursery school the signs of problems cannot be perceived and dealt with (Manning and Herrmann, 1981). Even at very young ages, children's difficulties with friendship can be spotted by observant adults and correctional guidance, training or treatment can be started. For example, a problem child is particularly noticed by teachers as one who very rarely initiates a conversation with them, or who quarrels and fights often, fails to cope with opposition from other children in a satisfactory manner, and makes overly demanding approaches to other children. Such children are very often noticeably unhappy or liable to sharp changes in mood. Something more serious actually lies behind this troublesome behaviour although it is not only inexperienced or unperceptive teachers and parents who fail to appreciate this. The pattern may mean something as serious as the onset of a clinical or psychiatric disorder, or may merely mean the beginning of a development towards deviancy of some kind. Relationships at nursery schools in the 3-5-year-old range are thus likely to affect the child's whole future just as much as the relationships with parents do; but they depend on different things and concern different areas of development — particularly, at these ages, developments in beliefs about friendship.

Such developments are quite dramatic (La Gaipa, 1981). Very young children (2½-4 years) describe other people and their value as friends in terms of concrete characteristics (e.g. 'John is my friend because he lives in a big house'). Later, in early childhood, children use more personalised descriptions ('John is my friend because he is tough'), but do not use psychologically evaluative descriptions of the sort familiar to adults (e.g. 'John is a friend because he is a nice, helpful, thoughtful person'). By later childhood (say age eight years) friends are seen as people who share joint activities, provide help and support against enemies, are able to produce practical assistance and often provide physical benefits. Here is the first time when the admiration of a friend's character begins to feature in children's descriptions of friends, but it is only right at the point where childhood turns into adolescence (around twelve years) that friendship notions start to focus on intimate sharing, secrets, private knowledge, trust and loyalty, genuineness and acceptance of the friends, warts and all.

The notion of disliking is also something that undergoes dramatic transformations with age (Gaebler, 1980). At the earliest ages dislike is expressed through behaviour, not through words: rejection and avoidance are the clearest methods. Children of about five will be able to express dislike for others, but do not give specific nor satisfactory reasons (e.g. 'I dislike him because I do' — a circular definition or, at best, something like 'I dislike him because he's horrid'). At this age, and right up until about eight years, the reasons that they give for disliking someone are not direct opposites of the reasons that they give for liking someone. They dislike people who fight or are rough, whilst they like people who give them sweets or play with them. Liking and disliking are not strict logical opposites for 8-year-olds. For this reason a child's likes and dislikes may not be particularly stable until mid- to late childhood, when the concepts begin to 'set', and the child forms a more complete and robust idea of the nature of friendship and its opposite. Once the ideas set — in the period of later childhood and adolescence — the learning that must then be done falls more squarely into the area of behavioural learning rather than learning of concepts or beliefs: that is, the young adolescent must start to learn and practise its newly acquired ideas about friendship.

All the same, there are several significant changes even in a younger child's behaviour towards other people as the child gets older and these are so systematic as to amount to a relatively 'normal' pattern, worth spending time considering here. One curiosity that may be important psychologically is that from about four up to the age of ten (and even a bit beyond in most cases) a child's friendship choices and the child's comments about friends and friendship are predominantly in relation to same-sex friends, and in relation to people the same age as itself (La Gaipa, 1981). Before the age of four the child has little enough idea of friendship (or of sexual differences if it comes to that: it takes time for them to appreciate that biological sex is a fixture and cannot be changed at a whim). After the age of ten the problem of creating and managing friendships with the opposite sex begins to be more significant. Of course, during adolescence such problems take up a large percentage of the person's time, although girls begin to get concerned about them well before most boys do.

So children probably learn most about friendship with same-sex people before the turmoil of adolescence takes them into the market-place of significant relationships with the opposite sex. In the first stages their friendship choices are not particularly stable, and loyalty to a friend is not much prized. Friends are people who do things for you, or give you things like sweets, as far as a 6-year-old is concerned. If someone unexpected does this for you one day, then they are pretty instantly labelled a friend and will as soon lose the crown tomorrow if they do not repeat the performance.

The apparently pointless quarrels, making up and changes of allegiance are actually quite important training grounds for children to do early learning about the management of relationships in general. Well-meaning parents are probably ill-advised to keep breaking up fighting children unless danger is imminent. More useful is not the outside influence of an adult, but advice and guidance subsequently about how the child should have handled the disturbance, the importance of considering other people's views, and the desirability of using means other than force to resolve disputes. But such advice must be made appropriate to the age of the child and to the child's development of understanding about friendship. Emphasis on sharing and co-operation will be more clearly understood, and hence more readily accepted, by an 8-year-old than will emphasis on loyalty, trust or the non-violation of confidences.

What else do children learn? As well as the learning of concepts relevant to friendship, they are learning, as they grow older, the various activities that are important in the actual conduct of social relationships. This is important for the obvious reason that what really matters is not simply how a child views friendship, but rather the ability to perform the activities of friendship in a way that is consistent with such views and with the general views held by the other children that they encounter. It is important that they learn what to do, what to say, and the value of co-operation, as well as how to quarrel and make up. They must also learn something along the way about their own social assets and their value to other people. They learn how other people characteristically respond to them —

and this can have an important effect on their view of themselves (their self-image), which can in turn influence their willingness to risk friendly or sociable activity.

Over and above this, the child is learning something about the nature of the social world and how to operate in it whilst it is increasing in social understanding and interpersonal skills (La Gaipa, 1981). As the understanding and concept of friendship matures, so are children's friendships more stable and persistent, although even at the ages of 10-13 the friendships are predominantly with same-sex partners. At this time (early adolescence) the child becomes more concerned about the reliability of a friend, the psychological and emotional support that a friend provides, and the confidences that are shared. Increasing emphasis is placed on the talking over of problems with friends and, as adolescence gets under way, there is a sudden surge of interest in the character, disposition and general psychological make up of other people. Until adolescence the individual's understanding of motivation is very primitive and there is little grasp of the complex reasons that people have for their actions. People's moods and dispositions are only crudely comprehended and such things as another person's emotional stability would play a very little role in the child's choice of that person as a friend.

The research also shows that children who are withdrawn or socially disabled usually also have a distorted view of friendship or else one that is far below what is appropriate for a child of their age (La Gaipa and Wood, 1981). Thus a child of nine may have a friendship 'age' of seven. It is not surprising that it then finds it hard to make friends with children its own age and so become socially withdrawn because there are usually physical and social barriers against befriending children outside their own age group. Such notions of friendship do not seem very clearly related to intelligence, and even bright children can sometimes be a bit backward in friendship terms. What seems to matter is the experience and the range of opportunities they have had to play with other children; possibly even before they went to school.

When parents or teachers suspect that a child has relational problems — which may come to light in obvious ways through persistent complaints from other children, or in less obvious ways through work problems, refusal to participate in games, or instability of moods and sleep patterns — the first requirement is an expert diagnosis of the level of the problem. If the child has general problems related to self-esteem then the correct solution to the problems lies in a different course of action from the one that is suitable if they are simply slow to develop appropriate concepts about friendship. If, on the other hand, the problem is centred on poor enactment of friendship skills and behaviours then the solution lies in the sorts of social skill training programmes and coaching efforts that have been successful in the USA, and are discussed below. However, before such drastic steps are taken, the parents and teachers should ask themselves what they can do to help. The most important but by far the simplest answer is that they should pay attention to the child's relationships with other people — with adults as well as with other children. It is important that the child draws useful lessons not only from quarrels but also from satisfactory interchanges. Even with an unproblematic child, the thoughtful parent will always underline the principle that a given interchange demonstrates (e.g. the benefits of sharing, the importance of co-operation with friends, the values of loyalty and trust, and so on). To some extent the child will find this unsatisfactory on its own because most of its practical experience will be derived from play with other children when parents are not there to see. However, just as with other sorts of learning and training, the point is to get the child to think for itself in new situations, using the principles that the parent or teacher is trying to instil.

Another simple point must also be made: not all children progress in social knowledge at the same rate. While the child will probably benefit from playing with very slightly older children who are more advanced, this is not necessarily the case. The research shows that children prefer friends who are at their own level of social development (or slightly above) but not usually those at a markedly lower level (La Gaipa, 1981). Thus while the less developed child may benefit from playing with the more developed child, the discrepancy may be large enough for the more advanced child to become uncomfortable, and so to turn the experience into a negative one for the underdeveloped child. When, on the contrary, the manipulation of such contexts for friendship is guided and co-ordinated by experts the effects are often very good. Several programmes in America have been devoted to exploring this particular avenue for social improvement (Furman, in preparation). In one type of case, problem children or socially-retarded children are introduced into carefully composed and structured groups and the experience itself helps them. In other cases they are carefully observed at play and are then 'debriefed' or talked through the experience by a trained researcher in a way that focuses them on their successes and on the points that they could improve (Asher and Gottman, 1981). Such training in sensitivity to the effects of their own behaviour seems to be particularly effective, but requires expert handling. A third method of intervention is to draw up a dictionary or conceptual map of the child's ideas about friendship and to retrain the child where such concepts are found to be inadequately developed (La Gaipa and Wood, 1981). These all work quite well once the child's problem has been correctly assessed.

However, the root problem is very likely to be related to self-esteem, and may require psychotherapeutic intervention in severe cases. In less severe cases, and in any case where the parent wants to avoid future problems, the parents and teachers should help the child to obtain or retain a reasonably high self-esteem by pointing out their successes in relationships, and helping to defuse or minimise the effect of negative social experiences. They should also make conscious efforts to encourage the child to think about friendship and to try to ponder its principles. Children need encouragement with their social conceptual development just as much as with other aspects of their intellectual development.

Given that researchers place great emphasis on the learning and development of conceptual understanding of friendship, their next most important concern is the behaviour of friendship, particularly the non-verbal behaviour that is involved (Furman, in preparation). There are consistent differences between popular and unpopular children not only in what they know or believe about friendship, but in how they conduct it and bring it to life. Popular children are more inclined to (and better able to) initiate play with other children, and presumably they become popular because of this. It just might be vice versa, although other studies suggest that once children are coached in the skills of starting play and friendship, so their popularity increases. There is generally thought to be a parallel between the behaviour of unpopular children and the behaviour of newcomers: that is, newcomers to a school show a particular style of behaviour for a while; unpopular children show it most of the time (Putallaz and Gottman, 1981). For instance, newcomers look the other children in the face when they play, and so do unpopular children; by contrast, acquaintances and friends look more at what they are playing with, or look around the room. As I indicated in chapter 2, looking at someone's face (as distinct from gazing at their eyes, specifically) is a usual way of expressing basic friendliness to new acquaintances, and demonstrates the fact that the relationship is an uncertain, starting one. Unpopular children are constantly signalling to other children that their relationship is an uncertain one, therefore. Unpopular children communicate ambivalence in other ways: they turn their backs on other children more often, they stand still rather than joining in the movements of other children, they 'automanipulate' more, that is, they play with their hair, scratch themselves, and so on. All of these behaviours are signs of doubt, insecurity and anxiety, and they are just as noticeable to other children as they are to observant adults (Putallaz and Gottman, 1981).

The most diagnostic difference between children who know how to be friends and those who do not is the specific problem known as 'hovering'. In hovering, the child lurks on the edge of a group, shows indecision about entering and joining in, decides to join in too late when the others are moving on to something else, and adopts a pleading, whining style of talking. Hoverers also show lower ability to concentrate; higher rates of daydreaming, and more frequent episodes of staring out into space. Such children are clearly disturbed. Furthermore, the behaviour is typical of some abused children and may indicate that such children 'invite' abuse in this way (perhaps partly explaining why often only one child in a family is abused). It has even been shown in some cases that when such an abused child is removed to a 'safe' foster home, the foster parents may also abuse the child, or request that it be removed because they cannot cope. It is therefore very important to spot the development of hovering and to do something about it. At the very

129

youngest ages parents and teachers may feel inclined to do little about it, but this can be an extremely unwise attitude, given the consequences that can follow from poor relationships in early childhood.

The basic problem here is a complicated one and it really lies beyond the layperson or concerned parent to correct it: what must be corrected and improved is the isolated or unpopular child's whole strategy for behaviour in friendship. Their behavioural strategy requires meticulous examination and systematic reconstruction. There are now several programmes in the USA for conducting such interactions, and although they are still at the experimental and development stage, success rates are very encouraging. A simple 4-week programme is enough to bring about behavioural changes that significantly increase the child's popularity (Oden and Asher, 1977). The programme consists of expert instruction about the initiation of friendly behaviour and entry into a group (e.g. participation, co-operation, helping, proper communication and non-verbal skills), opportunities to practise the skills and strategies in groups, and a review with the coach. The effects are not merely immediate, but also prolonged. In follow-up studies a year later the previously unpopular children were showing continued progress and had retained their new-found popularity.

Successful entry into a group is certainly a skill that needs practice when it is underdeveloped, but it is not the whole story. The child has to know what to do when it is accepted into the group, and has to adopt an effective strategy for staying in. Unpopular children are very often bossy and demanding, they disagree more with other children and get into argumentative struggles, and they talk about themselves much more often (Putallaz and Gottman, 1981). In short, they attempt to force the other children to pay attention to them, to the exclusion of other tasks, games and people. Programmes designed to remove this poor strategy can focus the children on ways of being more rewarding to other children rather than demanding attention from them. In some cases the changes are very minor but very effective: for instance, unpopular children are very specific in their instructions to other children and give no alternatives, whilst popular children cite a general rule and then offer alternative ways of fulfilling it. An example of the unpopular style might be: 'You can't move when you throw a six.' The popular child might say 'You aren't supposed to do that. You're supposed to pick up one of the cards.' Although these differences seem small, they actually build into the pattern that causes popularity and unpopularity.

In summary, unpopular children have low self-esteem, more psychological defences against rejection, poorly developed understanding of the meaning of friendship, an immature style of attempting to enter a group, and a poor and unacceptable behavioural strategy for conducting the activities of friendship. The differences between popular and unpopular children are often so seemingly trivial that they can easily be missed — yet they make the difference between success and failure in childhood relationships and, ultimately, between success and failure as an adult in society.

Growing from Childhood to Adolescence

The social learning and relational education of childhood is predominantly focused on friendships with other children of the same sex. It is only later in development that opposite-sex friendships become acceptable, desirable, important and worth the risks of trying. Up until the age of twelve or so, there is considerable group pressure not to play with (or express liking for) the opposite sex, and it is usually only popular children who risk it until quite late on. Adolescence thus brings not only intellectual, social and sexual changes: it also brings several changes of emphasis in relationships. All of the changes have sweeping consequences for friendship, both in adolescence itself and also in later adulthood, since it is in the turmoil of adolescence that many new inadequacies of friendship can be acquired and stamped in.

Many reasons can be found for the changes and for their consequences. First, the development in understandings about friendship continues and grows (Kon, 1981). Second, the adolescent begins to become capable of forming friendships in different ways from the ones that children find to be important: specifically, adolescents are increasingly concerned about the character of their friends, and place great emphasis on loyalty and trust in friendship. Third, adolescents begin to develop the adult concern over finding support for their personality and have to nourish the skills of detecting it and exploring its extent, as discussed in chapters 2 and 3. Errors and embarrassments in this task are as likely as successes with these entirely new experiences. Fourth, the adolescent becomes much more independent and much more responsible for the conduct and success of friendship. This requires the skills of forming and stage-managing relationships to a much greater extent than previously in childhood. An additional dimension is provided by the fact that many such relationships are not only with the opposite set but are sexual in nature. There begin the many complications of dating and courtship, the problems of handling sexual desires and restraints, and the difficulties of creating satisfactory relationships with members of the opposite sex. Finally, the difficulties of maintaining all sorts of relationship become much more significant once the child's timespan turns into the adolescent's and there is a greater appreciation of the fact that friendships last, sometimes for life.

For all these dramatic reasons early, middle and late adolescence are true test-beds for later adult relationshps and are likely breeding grounds for many sorts of personal disturbance that can persist right through adulthood (Duck, 1975). One important point here is that adolescence is really the first time that people become very clearly aware of differences in the degrees of friendship that can exist. A child will simply distinguish best friends from friends and the others — but an adult is able to distinguish many other more subtle different degrees of friendship, different types of friend (e.g. workmate, personal friend, neighbour) and different stages in the growth of friendship. Thus adults know that friendship progresses from first encounters with strangers, through casual acquaintanceship, to close friendship — and that it really takes time. A younger child will tend to believe that friendship is all or nothing; and they have little idea about a slow process of getting to know someone: you either are a friend or you are not.

One of the changes in later childhood and early adolescence is the more sophisticated view of the growth of friendship through different grades, and that these grades are based on what we know about the other person — how well we know them, indeed. Younger children do not think, as adolescents begin to do, about how much they know about someone, and about what they have yet to learn. Especially, children and adolescents are different in that the adolescents begin, as part of this change, to pay attention to other people's personality. As they gain an increasingly sophisticated view of the fact that people do have inner characteristics, personalities, moods, wishes, desires, motivations and intentions, so they begin to make increasing use of this realistion in the conduct of their social lives in general and their friendships in particular.

This, of course, means that they start the long business of making a personal dictionary of personality, or creating their own theory of what makes people tick (Duck, 1975). This means finding out the sorts of terms that best describe other people's characters, and testing out or becoming familiar with the use of these terms. They must test out their own abilities as judges of character and they must learn to find friends who really do have the qualities that they admire, as well as finding those people who can offer them the personal support that they need. These choices are also an early part of learning the process of managing and assuming greater personal responsibility for the conduct of one's personal relationships. Indeed, one source of conflict with parents is often the growing desire to choose and develop one's own friendships for oneself rather than through parents. Since this is an especially potent time for learning, mistakes are made — just as they are later — but because at this age it is especially important to the adolescent, strong stands are often taken and conflicts with parents usually result. Since it is important to adolescents to develop some control over their relationships, and since they do not yet do so on the same basis as adults, these conflicts may appear to parents to be irrational obstinacy. To the adolescent they are seen as fundamental to their independence. Both viewpoints are correct.

Boys, furthermore, are very likely to form into, or join, gangs at the early points of adolescence, causing their parents alarm although girls' cliques usually do not (Kon, 1981). However, these gangs and cliques are the basis for subsequent growth or normal sexuality since they give the young person a 'safe' base from which to run the risk of forming first relationships with the opposite sex. In very important ways they also act as rulemakers for normal behaviour. This is because, between them, the members create a 'theoretical' approach to relationships (in terms of beliefs, ideas and hopes) that actually creates the foundations of their relationships with the opposite sex later on. Parents who discourage their children from joining such gangs and cliques are probably preventing them from establishing the basis for normal adult relationships at the proper time.

It is a well-known feature of adolescent relationships that they characterise a time of movement (Kon, 1981). First, there is movement away from parents and adults in general towards their peers as the point of reference. For adolescents, the people in their age group gradually, but significantly, become much more central torchbearers of opinions and standards, with the ideas of parents and adults being rejected or derogated, almost as a matter of duty. Secondly, there is, as mentioned above, the movement away from predominantly same-sex friendships towards relationships and friendships with the opposite sex. These changes have their psychological effects as well as their relational ones. Adolescents who are deprived of casual, friendly interactions with their peers are going to have trouble developing a normal personality at a normal rate, since personality testing and growth is a major result of adolescent friendship and gang membership. If such developments do not take place then it becomes increasingly difficult for the adolescent to enter relationships that require that development first; and so a vicious circle is entered.

These are obvious and clear movements, but there are some less obvious ones too, for instance the subtle movement, mentioned above, from pair friendships to gang or clique friendships (La Gaipa, 1981). Instead of having the one, two or three best friends of a normal child, normal adolescents rapidly absorb themselves into larger clusters which provide many sorts of psychological support and many sorts of psychological guidance or prescription. Each gang develops its own views about what should be done and what should not, and its own attitudes about relationships with other people, especially the opposite sex. These gangs and cliques introduce the adolescent forcibly to different features of friendship since they often exert sanctions upon members of the gang who do not form the right sort of friendships or the right number. Equally, the cliques present the individual with the forceful social implications of his place in the hierarchy of the group. Gangs and cliques invariably evolve a structure which can develop or restrain the individual's growth. For instance, the leaders and high status members of the gang or clique are always the first ones who are 'permitted' to start friendships with the opposite sex whilst low status members are ridiculed or ostracised if they attempt such friendships. Particularly, the male adolescent must therefore first prove himself to his same-sex peers before they will tolerate his attempting to find companions of the opposite sex.

Thus, besides the other things being learned by the adolescent, are the significance of status, the force of group pressure, the significance of disobeying the group rules or norms for behaviour, and the tragic inter-relationship of status and success with opposite-sex friends. Partly as a result of direct influence from the group, and partly as a consequence of indirect cues from media such as TV, comics and pop group fan clubs, the adolescent begins to be 'shaped' with respect to beliefs about the types of other person who are most desirable as friends and the degree of emotional involvement that should be expected or displayed in friendship.

The adolescent is also continually developing and evolving a more sophisticated language of friendship — a broader and deeper system of concepts to apply to relationships with other people and what to expect or extract from them. In particular, the adolescent develops the idea that people are not simply sources of gratification of the person's own needs but have requirements and needs of their own (La Gaipa and Wood, 1981). The normal adolescent thus changes from demanding of others to being demanded of, and from being provided for to providing for others. Because this requires a dramatic shift in perspective, and because it brings the adolescent face to face with his ability to provide for others' demands, it is usually experienced as complex, confusing and threatening. Instead of concerning themselves with what other people can offer them, adolescents must find what they have to offer other people. This can generate confusion, alienation and the severest self-doubts. It is one of many reasons why adolescents discuss and argue about friends and friendship more than children do.

When the Lessons are not Learned

This can all be summed up very simply: first, the adolescent learns to expect different things of friends from those that children expect; second, the adolescent learns that different people are significant in defining friendship (i.e. peers do it, now, not adults); third, the adolescent learns to communicate differently to friends and learns to learn about friendship and its development through stages.

The biggest risks are that the adolescent does not complete all of these lessons satisfactorily. Of course, the differences between levels of social development in children that were mentioned earlier do not simply disappear because the child has become an adolescent. Some adolescents are more socially advanced than others of the same calendar age. Significantly, adolescents — particularly girls — begin to show a preference for friends who are older, whilst children almost invariably choose friends of the same age as themselves, give or take a few months. Adolescents hardly ever (about 4 per cent of all cases) pick same-sex friends who are significantly younger than themselves — say in the year below them at school (Kon, 1981).

For the same reason that it is beneficial for younger children to play with slightly older children, the adolescents probably find it rewarding to have relationships with slightly more advanced adolescents because these, as it were, show them the ways in which they should grow psychologically. That is to say, adolescents who form friendships only with younger persons may be retarding themselves developmentally, or may be slightly socially retarded in the first place. It should be a useful sign that something is amiss when parents notice their adolescent showing a marked preference for friendship with much younger persons.

Mildly retarded social development is only one reason why an adolescent may develop friendships that are not only ultimately unsatisfying, but are also predictive of probable dissatisfaction with later adult relationships (La Gaipa and Wood, 1981). For one thing, adolescence brings to fruition the curse of an in-adequately supportive family or a disturbed childhood where trust in other people could not be established. Individuals who have no history of basic trust in relationships with other people will have more than the usual uphill struggle to establish friendships based on the criterion of trust in adolescence: they have little encouragement to draw on from past experience.

Equally, many disturbed and socially withdrawn adolescents have already acquired a highly negative view of the value of social relationships, and are very wary of other people (La Gaipa and Wood, 1981). They tend to 'use' them, and are primarily help-seekers rather than help-givers — which, of course, makes them relatively less attractive to their potential partners and so less likely to be invited into relationships with other people. Other adolescents are difficult to relate to because they maintain an immature or aggressive style of behaviour that the other people find unattractive or hard to cope with. These adolescents are likely to find it hard to maintain friendships, whilst the 'users' are likely to find it hard to develop them in the first place.

Just as popular and unpopular children show characteristic differences in ability to begin and continue relationships, so disturbed and normal adolescents show characteristic differences in their approaches to the development and maintenance of friendship (La Gaipa and Wood, 1981). Normal adolescents focus on the possibilities of self-development through friendship; that is, they do as described earlier, and select friends who help them to develop their personality. By contrast, disturbed adolescents focus on their perceptions of their own inadequacy and on doubts that the friend really values them. For instance they have excessive doubts about their own personal worth as friends for other people, and assume that other people are their friends out of pity. Accordingly, a normal adolescent focuses on the skills and abilities of the other person, whilst the disturbed adolescent focuses questioningly on the other person's genuineness. Such suspicion and doubt are sure to make it harder for other people to relate to the disturbed adolescent, and hence to increase the doubts about genuineness.

As in the case of unpopular children, so too with adolescents it is the case that the warning signs can be picked up by observant adults and used to help the adolescent towards a more satisfactory use of the skills of friendship. It must be honestly admitted that psychological research has not been funded here as it ought to be, and the number of correctional programmes is correspondingly underdeveloped. Programmes in Canada have been concerned with the problem of integrating the disturbed adolescent into the normal group and have explored the ways in which disturbed adolescents are perceived by normal adolescents (La Gaipa and Wood, 1981). We can be sure, however, that a root problem is the disturbed adolescents' beliefs about friendship and the behaviour that they base on the beliefs. Intervention programmes based on those that are successful in children would also work in the case of disturbed adolescents. They would require modification to suit adolescent needs and are probably beyond the skills of most schools.

It is disturbing to have to admit that education of children and adolescents about friendship has been so thoroughly under-researched through lack of support, despite the importance of both childhood and adolescence as seed-beds for society's future problems. We should perhaps take more trouble to explore what goes wrong with adult relationships and build upon what we know about child development in order to prevent children's problems turning into adult ones. (The next chapter looks at deficient relationships.) But the consequences of poor childhood learning about friendship can be very severe and this is an area where prevention is better than cure. It is best to catch possible problems early, before they have burned themselves irresistibly into the individual's psyche. There seems little reason to doubt that our society's social and psychological 'casualty departments' are unnecessarily full of lonely people who can be helped by training programmes. Yet such training programmes, based on a clearer idea of what actually does go wrong when childhood (and adult) relationships fail, are beginning to be devised. They show the promise of being able to put satisfactory relationships within the grasp of more and more people who are unhappy as a result of their poor childhood relationships.

Summary

This chapter deals with a key issue: namely, where do an adult's friendships start — indeed, where does all their relational behaviour originate? In short, the chapter explores social relations in childhood and adolescence. I have stressed the importance (in early childhood) of the development of a level of self-esteem.

This has to be high enough to create and encourage a person's desires for relationships with other people, and people who develop low self-esteem in childhood will be less able to make friends as adults. In later childhood the main emphasis of the learning falls on the development of satisfactory concepts of friendship. Each child has to learn what friendship involves, and has to come to beliefs that match up with those held by peers and children in the surrounding social environment. Although dramatic changes in the conceptual basis for understanding and dealing with friendships are still occurring, the major area of relational learning in adolescence focuses on the *management* of relationships. Adolescents have to learn proper ways of behaving in, and conducting, friendships — particularly romantic friendships with the opposite sex. At all times in the chapter I have stressed the fundamental importance of such learning about friendships: a young person's learning about relationships sets the pattern for their future adult friendships: there are no two ways about it.

6

Poor Relations

Many of us make the mistake of believing that people who cannot form relationships must have something wrong with them. Indeed, we sometimes reject or ignore lonely people for the very reason that they are lonely — which makes them socially dangerous to associate with because they may 'infect' our own reputation. We do not wish to be seen by other people as incapable of attracting anyone except lonely social outcasts looking for somewhere to park; so most people leave them alone. This is not only unfortunate for them, it may actually be dangerous. Many independent investigators are now sure that loneliness and loss of friends cause all sorts of illness, both psychological and physical. This is certainly true at the simple level that lonely people often become neglectful of themselves and less caring about their appearance, diet or health. Many recluses simply do not take any care of themselves at all, and exist in foolish, thoughtless, self-destructive ways almost as if they are hell-bent on punishing themselves.

However, there are many other more serious effects of isolation and loneliness. For example, it has been found time and time again that many coronary patients have small friendship networks and, conversely, that 'loners' are more likely to have heart attacks (Lynch, 1977). It is also found that loners tend to adopt a pattern of work that creates more health problems, often overworking and developing illnesses that are presently known to derive from stress. The point here is a simple one: it is no use trying to cure stress patterns if we ignore one of the most significant contributors: friendship problems.

There are many examples of disease caused by relational

disturbances. For instance, people whose marriages break up are vastly more likely to develop severe stress-related illnesses such as ulcers, bad headaches, disruption of sleep, high anxiety and circulatory problems. They also have more driving accidents, higher suicide rate, and more problems with alcohol (Bloom, *et al.*, 1978). It is not simply due to 'worry', as many people would superficially suppose, because people with other worries do not show exactly the same pattern of disease. It is because people with breaking marriages are experiencing the break up of all the supports and functions that the close marriage or friendship provides. They are entering a minefield of psychological threat without the support of their customary guide.

Another way to sum up this state of affairs is to say that there is absolutely no doubt that while good relations have a powerful positive effect on people, it is depressingly clear that poor relations have an equally impressive negative effect. Yet although psychosomatic effects in medicine have been known for some time, it is only quite recently that people have looked on the influence of personal relationships in the equation. It is as if we all knew that the mind could affect the body, but that we have only just realised the ways in which personal relationships affect the mind. It does seem a bit odd at first sight to propose that we need friends to stay healthy — even though there has been plenty of apparently unrelated evidence around for a long time to support the idea. For instance, we knew that depression could make people lose the will to live; we also knew that loss of friends could make people depressed. Now research has added it all up and shown that relationship disturbance may be the first link in a chain that leads to fatal illness. Once that is recognised, both individuals and society at large need to do their utmost to avoid or correct the problems caused by loneliness and poor relations.

What I have been trying to emphasise in this book is that likeability and unlikeability cannot be explained just in terms of the attractive or unattractive qualities that someone has. People who are ugly, arrogant, silly, diseased, greasy or foolish often have many friends. For instance, Socrates was noted as ugly and yet had many close friends; Julius Caesar was high-handed, bald and lecherous and yet his soldiers liked him; and Martin

Luther suffered from various unpleasant digestive problems but was well-liked. The deep causes of likeability and unlikeability are quite simply to do with performance, behaviour and action. The behaviours and processes that happen once meeting has occurred — those are what make or break a relationship and those are what are responsible for good or bad relationships. In short, people will tolerate a smelly extravert, but not a beautiful social cripple. This is a good thing: it means that people with poor relationships can be helped or can help themselves to try out and experiment with new ways of conducting their friendships.

It should now be clear that there are very many different reasons why someone may behave incorrectly in friendship. For one thing, as the previous chapter showed, a person may retain an immature understanding of what friendship is. Quite simply, he may mistake the activities involved (e.g. sharing of goods but not of secrets; physical support not psychological support) when these are appropriate only to childish friendships. Or he may have failed, as an adolescent, to learn the fundamental importance of trust and confidence-keeping in friendship. These people have a poorly developed idea of what friendship means to normal adults, and they will do the wrong things simply because their guiding principles are faulty. They may get on very well with children, but adults will find them hard to cope with and hard to form close relationships with. As indicated in the previous chapter, such problems can be dealt with once people know how to recognise them and learn what they mean.

A second reason why someone may behave ineptly in friendship is also to do with problematic development as children — but a different sort of developmental problem. Because of early experiences people sometimes develop constricted personalities or low self-esteem. Such people become suspicious of other people, are hostile and aggressive, or may be so neurotic that no one can cope with them as friends. Their concept of friendship may be perfectly all right but they, as personalities, are not. Obviously, the solution to poor friendships would be different in the case of people like this from how it would be for people who didn't know what adult friendships ought to be like. Treatment for these people will be basically psychotherapeutic, and based on open, warm encouragement to trust other people in friendship. Treatment for the other type will consist of guidance about the nature of friendship and specific training or education by specially designed programmes.

A third reason why people may behave incorrectly in friendship could be that they lack the skills of friendship outlined in previous chapters. This reason is much more common than most people realise, and part of the problem is that it can take highly specialised forms. By this I mean that some people may suffer from 'skill deficit' only in some types of relationships (e.g. with the opposite sex) and not in others (e.g. with children or same-sex people). Other people may be skilled at beginning relationships, but may lack the skills to develop them or, worse, to sustain and keep them. Yet others may be very good at establishing quick, superficial relationships with strangers, but may be unable to cope with lasting, deeper, and more personally intimate relationships. For instance, they may feel threatened, vulnerable and exposed when they begin to realise that their friend is getting to know their personality very well; they fear that what the friend will discover may not be liked.

It is difficult to know which of these deficits is the most frustrating for the persons involved. Obviously all of them are serious, all of them cause major psychological and emotional distress, each of them is differently caused and requires different treatment which can be carried out by the person himself and only some of which require special counselling. To help draw this distinction, compare these two letters I have received. One, from 'Alfred', shows how disturbing it is to be unable to start friendships (and also, I believe, shows us some of the reasons why Alfred had no friends. Look at the short, sharp sentences and the off-putting style).

Dear Dr Duck,

I'm in need of help and would like to know if you can help me. I'm 25-years-old and totally unable to make friends with other people. I find it difficult to talk and what to talk about. I become very nervous and self-conscious. All my communications are short, straightforward. What I think is known as small talk. Up to now, I haven't mixed with people because of being unable to talk. I don't have any friends. Beside being born a quiet, shy chap, I had a very religious, sheltered life. Because of this I become very self conceited and pompous. Please can you help me. Thanks.

Yours sincerely,
'Alfred'

The other letter was from 'Madge', and her complaint was about poor development of relationships. She shows a sensitivity to the problems, whilst being unable to find solutions.

Dear Dr Duck,

I am one of those people who does not seem able to make friends and I get so disheartened at times because I do not know how to change this.

I meet people at the office and I enrolled in F.E. evening classes, I joined a knitting circle and a year ago in conjunction with another woman, started a local group of N.H.R. to give myself the opportunity of meeting people. Somehow I never seem to get past the initial stage of getting to know them, I dry up at asking questions about themselves for fear they think I am prying so that doesn't make me feel very easy in their company. I try to be friendly and obliging towards people, nevertheless, in the hope that I can cover up my unease. It gives me such an inferiority complex that I now stammer slightly too.

Unfortunately, my husband is a very quiet person who does not feel the need for company very often so I don't really make friends through this source. We have a lot of acquaintances through our work and neighbours, etc., and I do try so hard to get on with everyone but I don't ever seem to get to know them any better. The few people I do get to know don't seem to want to get very friendly, maybe it is because they don't really find me their type of person? — I don't know.

I know through these sources that people see me as a friendly, lively and confident sort of person and it baffles me all the more that I can't make friends. I am a hypersensitive person and find myself very aware of the subtle changes in people's moods towards me and I find it confusing when people 'go off' me for no apparent reason.

I appeal for your help, Dr Duck, and would very much appreciate a reply.

Yours sincerely,

'Madge'

I believe that these two letters make some important points about poor relations, and they emphasise that when relationships are unsatisfactory or go sour the correct course of action is to examine the *processes* that happen in them, rather than to try and find which of our personal characteristics needs changing. New hairstyles, new clothes and plastic surgery are less important than a new way of looking at the problems, and a new way of behaving. For instance, recent studies show that many people with relationships difficulties blame themselves rather than looking at the situation they are in, and how it might limit their opportunities for relationships. Yet there are many natural limits to growth of relationships, and it makes sense for people to bear them in mind as a way of keeping a proper perspective on their success and failures in friendships. The next section considers a few of these, and it is a good idea for people to check through the list before they blame themselves and come to see the situation as permanent and unchangeable.

'Where did I go wrong?'

The problem here is that people demand explanations for their relationship's break up, and they are soon satisfied with some very unrealistic answers. It is all too natural — but not necessarily right just because it is natural — for people with a dissolving marriage or friendship to focus on themselves and ask themselves over and over again, 'What's wrong with me?' and 'Where did I go wrong?' The answers are more than likely to be 'Nothing' and 'You didn't'. It is a very well-known finding in psychology (since Heider, 1958) that people actually prefer personal explanations for things rather than external, situational or circumstantial explanations. We all like to blame persons rather than chance; we all tend to see things in personal terms rather than in terms of 'It just happened'. So personal sorts of explanation are given for the most unlikely things. The first time this tendency was examined was nearly forty years ago when a researcher showed people a cartoon of triangles and circles

145

moving around the screen. Observers preferred to describe it in personal terms: 'The triangle is chasing the circle, and the circle is running away because it is afraid'! There is every reason to believe that this human tendency prevails in poor relations, too. When things go wrong in a relationship people look for a person as a scapegoat — themselves or their friends.

Although human beings have this natural tendency to look for people to blame, or for persons rather than circumstances as the main cause of events, psychologists have for a long time regarded this as a fundamental error, particularly in respect of friendship and relationships. Humans are naturally tuned up to seek out personal causes for relationship difficulties, and to overlook the contribution of other causes. Yet there are many other reasons why relationships fail or do not reach their full potential, and most of them have very little to do with the people personally. For instance, two friends may simply live too far away for the best relationship to be conducted: if my best friends lived in Cleveland, Ohio or Boulder, Colorado and I live in Lancaster, England, then there are naturally going to be some dissatisfactions and some constraints in the relationships, even if they are enjoyable and satisfying as far as possible in the circumstances. As another example, there are some natural limits to relationships created by norms or public standards. The relationships possible between a teacher and pupil, boss and worker, or Queen and subject are naturally limited by expectations about what is proper in the circumstances, even if, in other circumstances, a deeply fulfilling relationship would be possible. As a third instance, recall from chapter 4 that individuals may have different expectations about the relationship and these differences may disrupt the relationship for reasons that do not fully reflect personally or badly on either partner. In focusing on these and on deficiencies of skill in friendship, I hope to re-emphasise as often as possible the fact that a relationship's breakdown can have many types of cause, and it is a mistake to focus on only one and to blame oneself too reproachingly. The first step towards correcting the problems is to take the new perspective provided by realisation of this fact.

People sometimes miss this point because the ending of relationships is usually tainted with self-accusations and guilt. It is perfectly normal but rather misguided for people in troubled relationship to start asking awkward questions about it (Duck, 1982). They start to question the relationship itself, most likely, and to ask whether they really need it and why. Unfortunately, because it is usually very difficult to answer this sort of question even when a relationship is going well, answers are particularly unsatisfying. The reasons for liking someone are hard enough to state verbally, even when there are no doubts that good reasons exist. Yet if there are any doubts at all then good and persuasive reasons for staying in the relationship are even harder to find. Also, as soon as individuals focus on a relationship, the lack of equity and fairness in exchange can soon become apparent (and is seen out of all proportion). It is easy to forget that in a properly developed relationship strict equity would not be expected anyway. So it is naturally very easy — but may be very wrong — to give it as the reason for a poor relationship, whether it actually is or not!

Plenty of research has shown that the tendency to give personal reasons for a break up is a shortsighted as a tendency as it is an inaccurate one (see Duck, 1982). Relationships break up for all sorts of reasons that people overlook or tend to blame on themselves when they are not responsible. Equally, they tend to overlook the possible influence of their personal *style* of behaviour, rather than specific events. For instance, a large amount of research has shown consistent sex differences in approaches to relationships and their dissolution (e.g. Hill *et al.*, 1976). Females are much more vigilant in relationships: that is, they watch the progress of relationships more carefully, are more concerned about the development of them, are more aware of disruptive undercurrents, think more often of the possibility of a friendship's ending, and are more likely to give sophisticated and complex accounts for the break up of a relationship than men are. In dating and courtship, the female partner is directly responsible for the breaks that occur in about 80 per cent of cases. Females fall in love move slowly, and yet fall out of love more quickly than men.

There are also some other influences on courtship and friendship that people would not usually think of: namely, time and the calendar. For example, in the northern hemisphere at any rate more marriages break up in February than any other month. Also, counsellors and social workers report every year that the period around and just after Christmas in Britain is one where marriage and family disturbances suddenly increase, probably because people are forced into stereotyped harmony and togetherness that does not really reflect their true feelings for one another. The media portrayals of closeness and conviviality simply, in many instances, contrast with the reality. Evidently the season of goodwill does not extend universally to one's next of kin.

Another interesting research finding is that the biggest risk time for courtships is around 15-18 months (Levinger, 1979). Many more are reported to run into trouble about this time than would be expected by chance. It seems likely that this is the sort of length of time that it takes most people to 'notice' the relationship, and to see that there is a clear expectation that it will end in marriage. When the partners come to the realisation — and, possibly more important, when outsiders do too, and begin to put pressure on them to clarify their intentions — the partners need to decide what their intentions really are. Presumably, then, there are many couples who decide that the time is not right, that it would be too early to commit themselves, that their careers are not well enough clarified — and a whole host of other reasons for deciding to call it off, rather than live out a hopeful but misleading life.

Other subtle reasons for break up can also be found. For instance, the break up of marriage will usually be blamed on the behaviour of one of the partners in the marriage, or upon the partners' behaviour with one another (sexual incompatibility, arguments, and so on). But it is a remarkable fact that a very substantial number of marriages break up about 8-10 years in. When researchers tend to explain this in terms of the length of the relationship and the strains that are created they have missed one key point: after 8-10 years of marriage most people, given the age at which people marry in the first place, are approaching the early mid-30s and are thus entering one of the well-known periods of psychological turmoil known as an 'identity crisis' — that is, the individual begins to feel the disappearance of youth, the greater fixity of life's probable career, and the closing of opportunities that would have still been open five years ago. (For example, in a lot of professions people are regarded as too old to join after the age of twenty-eight — in computing, officer training in the armed services, banking, and so on. People of this age are thus forced to recognise that certain paths are now closed.) It seems likely that many such people feel uneasy with their personal position, and simply give vent to this in the easiest place: their marriage or their personal relationships.

In developing friendships there are some hidden effects of 'length of time in the relationship' also, since, after about 4-6 months of friendship, people begin a very dramatic increase in the testing out of their relationship (McCarthy and Duck, 1976). For instance, they may have found that their friend is very similar to themselves in many attitudes — and they begin to wonder if the similarity is sincere. So they start trying out a few of their more outrageous views, just to see if the other person *dis*agrees. If so, then they may conclude that previous agreements were genuine rather than merely ingratiating.

People at this time try other tests too. For instance, they may try to find out whether their partner is likely to be stimulating, is capable of broadening them out in attitudes or opinions, or knows about things they have no knowledge of (Wright, 1982). Such tests are perfectly normal, useful and valuable ways of finding out the future value of a friendship but, of course, many relationships fail the test and break up. People begin to assert themselves more, to 'be themselves' rather than be polite in the friendship, they seek out areas of disagreement and attempt to resolve them vigorously. It does not always work and so the relationship crumbles. So, again, relationships can head towards the rocks because of the way everyone starts to behave in a relationship of that length. It is nothing personal if the friendship does not survive the test. That, after all, is the purpose of the test in the first place — to see if the friendship can survive, and is worthwhile for both partners to pursue. It is as healthy and beneficial for dying relationships to be discarded at this stage as it is for the healthy ones to be continued.

I have found other apparently wild effects of the calendar among students (Duck and Miell, 1981). In their first year at college (starting in October, of course) the Christmas break at the end of the first term seems to cement more of their college relationships that would be expected. The students go home looking forward to seeing their old schoolfriends, but get appalled and dismayed at the changes that have taken place in themselves and their friends at home. They find it harder to relate to them than they had expected, and come back to college in January feeling bursts of relief at meeting their college friends again. Students aren't the only ones who find it hard to keep up relationships with old friends from way back. Meetings between such people are often a bit hollow and the greater joy is usually to be found at the beginning and end of the meeting rather than in the middle.

All this serves to make the point that friendships often break up from the influence of strange and unlikely impersonal causes that people overlook. Few people stare at their partners and think, 'Hum! February again — perhaps we ought to break it all off' — but for some reason this is what seems to happen! It is very important that, recognising these strange effects that the research has thrown up, people whose relationships break up should keep a sense of perspective and not punish themselves as a first step. It may well be that their behaviour did contribute to the break up in a major way, but this need not be an untested assumption; rather, it should be a conclusion in context. In order to cope with the break up it is obviously intelligent to identify, as far as possible, the real causes of it, rather than to thrash around in speculative self-approach. Equally, the first step towards repairing a relationship is to identify as clearly as possible the true mix of personal and situational causes in the problems with the relationship.

Another point should also be made: not all relationships that break up are to be regretted. We must learn not only how to avoid breakdown of relationships when we wish to, but also how to welcome it when it is best to do so. It is folly to suggest that all breakdown of relationships is necessarily bad. Obviously there are cases where people sit down together and make a rational and calculated decision to break up the relationship. This is not because just one of them is now thoroughly unhappy or dissatisfied with the friendship, but because they both agree that they have reached the limits of what they can provide for one another. Or maybe they feel that the relationship is stifling their personal growth, or simply that it has gone as far as it is going and is now dead. Recent work in America has, indeed, uncovered the structure of ways in which people describe their burst relationships (McCall, 1982). A very elaborate system of metaphors applies to relationships and these have a very important role in convincing people that their relationship has ended or should end. For example, people who saw themselves as 'fellow travellers along life's highway' might come to see themselves as reaching a parting of the ways; people who saw themselves as providing each other with support like timbers, come to think of the collapse of the relationship. There is also a whole dictionary of metaphors related to coupling and uncoupling — 'getting hitched', 'stuck on one another', 'magnetically attracted', and so on — which imply that, once connected, two people can simply become disconnected, or the connections can become restraining: bonds can become chains. Finally, once people begin to want to leave relationships they use a characteristic style of language to describe the relationship, such as images of confinement ('I felt smothered', 'I was cooped in', 'It was like being in a cage'). Such differences of language and description are more significant than we normally appreciate, and they give an observant counsellor or confidant an immediate clue about the best strategy for counsel. Someone who uses imagery based on bonding is tacitly complaining that the closeness or lack of closeness in the relationship is the trouble, rather than anything else. Someone who complains of confinement is tacitly admitting that social pressures are the force that keeps the relationship together rather than strong emotional bonds. It is important for counsellors and confidants to pay close attention to such 'trivial' clues since they identify the person's focus on the problem, and may indicate that it is better to assist the person out of the relationship rather than to stick a big adhesive plaster over the problem. So some endings of relationships can actually be good, normal, and beneficial, as this helps the partners to grow, and stops their being suffocated.

Even when a break up is not mutually arranged, I do not want to suggest that this necessarily shows general unattractiveness or inadequacy. Nor do I wish to suggest that *any* ending of relationships is necessarily a bad reflection on the personal worth of the individuals concerned: they may just be doing something inappropriately without realising it — and it can be corrected, either by themselves personally, by their friends and acquaintances or by counsellors.

Coping with Poor Relations

That said, and the influence of non-personal factors clearly underlined, what can be done for individuals whose relationships are persistently unsatisfactory? Several strategies have already been outlined, and I shall focus here on the psychological adjustments that are possible before I look at the changes in behaviour that are effective.

First, consider the idea that someone feels isolated or feels that his relationships are unsatisfactory. When we explore what this actually means, it is perhaps best represented as the feeling that results when there is a discrepancy between two ideas that people may have about relationships (Perlman and Peplau, 1981). One of these ideas is a belief about the number of satisfactory relationships that they actually have, and the other is the level of desire or aspiration that they have for other people's company. Each of these will be different for different people, and what counts is the way in which each person sees them tying together. For instance, some people have a generally very low desire for other people's company, and so would not feel lonely if in fact they had a low number of satisfactory relationships. Other people with higher aspirations would feel terribly lonely with the exact same number of friends as this first person. People's desire for company and their perception of their present relationships are both changeable from time to time. Some days even normally sociable people just want to be alone and do so without geting morbid or upset. The problem and the pain arise when the discrepancy between beliefs about one's actual number of relationships and one's desired number of relationships is intolerably large and persistent.

Research has uncovered two psychological strategies that are effective in coping (Perlman and Peplau, 1981). In one the person adjusts his behaviour or attitudes towards the number of relationships that he actually has. For example, he may go out to create more relationships by meeting more people; or he may visit existing friends more often and for longer priods of time; or he may satisfy himself that he is underplaying himself and actually has more friends than he first thought, and that his existing friendships are actually very satisfying; or he may make so-called 'surrogate relationships', by buying a dog, talking to the television newsreaders, or replaying his memories of successful relationships that he had in the past. These methods can be very successful in adjusting attitudes to the relationships that people actually have. In the other method of coping, people adopt the strategy of adjusting their attitudes about the number of friendships that they desire. For instance they begin to see themselves as self-sufficient, independent 'loners'; or they can create an image of themselves in their own minds as independent, or someone who is happiest with one very close friend, or with the marriage partner, and insisting that this person provides all the psychological company they need. There is also the tendency for people to derogate other persons as friends ('You can't trust people, they always let you down') or to sublimate by non-sociable means like writing lots of letters to national organisations or, in extreme cases, by hallucinating about imaginary friends, visitors from outer-space, and contacts with spirits. Finally, they may simply take steps to alleviate the negative impact of loneliness, by, for instance, taking drugs, getting drunk or committing suicide.

These extreme responses have actually confused many people for a long time. For instance, it used to be noted that many alcoholic husbands reported poor sexual relationships with their wives and people jumped to the obvious, but wrong, conclusion: too much alcohol hinders sexual performance, and that was the cause of their poor sexual relationships. But it was also known that alcoholics often reported difficulties with other relationships, too, and again people jumped to an obvious but wrong conclusion: it was because alcoholism makes you difficult to live with. Nevertheless, when researchers began to look into it a bit deeper, they found that poor interpersonal relationships had often preceded the alcoholism (Orford and O'Reilly, 1981). Many leading researchers now believe that at least some alcoholics turned to alcohol as a refuge and anaesthetic against the effects of social isolation or chronically unsatisfying friendships. As in many other instances, the social isolation is a consequence of poor performance in friendmaking, and part of the cure for some alcoholics is to be found in improved relationships.

Equally, many family therapists are coming to the view that although the individuals in the family may have psychological disorders or difficulties, it is the relationship within the family and between the individuals that may provoke or aggravate them (see Orford and O'Reilly, 1981). It is occasionally found in very extreme cases (e.g. some types of schizophrenia) that the relationships in the individual's family are conducted in a rather peculiar way, and that the schizophrenia may result from this rather than cause it. Families containing difficult children or disruptive individuals are now often treated as family units rather than as if they were a lot of outsiders in a group with just one difficult member. The poor relationships in the family can often be bad enough to provoke one individual to burst out in dramatic ways and the cure is to treat and 'cure' the family not just the individual. For instance, an individual's disruptive behaviour may be partly determined or reinforced by the reactions of other family members, and it is no use giving therapy to the individual if the family merely reacts to the individual in the same old way once he returns from the therapy. The answer is to examine and investigate the patterns of activity and styles of interaction in the family as a whole — to take the family as a system with a malfunction rather than to isolate one component.

As further examples of the severe consequences of chronic faulty performance in friendships and other personal relationships, many forensic psychologists point to the fact that violent offenders often have a history of unsatisfactory relationships (Howells, 1981). This is particularly true of 'one-off' murderers (who, contrary to popular belief, are much more likely to kill a friend or family member than a stranger) and so-called 'murder-suicides', who kill someone very close to them (their spouse or child, most probably) and then kill themselves. In these cases it is commonly found that they are people who do not express their emotions. They bottle up their anger, cannot show affection except extremely (e.g. in violent sexual passion), and so on. Such people often 'burst' in unexpected ways, and other people are shocked because they do not see it coming in the gradual ways that would be expressed by people with normal ways of showing different degrees of emotion in their relationships. When they are treated for relationship difficulties their other symptoms subside. Such treatment usually involves training in normal expression of emotions. However it may also be the case that such persons inadvertently create the relationship bed that they lie on, and this style needs changing, too: for example, someone who is persistently aggressive and competitive may inadvertently organise other people to be hostile towards him or her, thus making the perceptions of hostility actually realistic. Such organising can readily be altered once the person is brought to the full realisation of the effects of their own behaviour on other people in the situation.

As a final example of the unlikely consequences of relationship problems, I recall reading in the local paper a story entitled 'Sex attack youth (18) jailed for six years'. In essence, an 18-year-old youth had threatened two women with an air pistol and attempted to embrace them — an act that the papers and prosecution represented as a 'sex attack'. In his defence the youth argued that he had no girlfriends, found relationships difficult, and only wanted someone to talk to. He claimed to have taken the pistol along in order to make the girls talk to him. He was found guilty and jailed for six years. I have often wondered if he is not really serving time because he did not know how to make friends or attract the opposite sex in the usual, understandable and acceptable ways. If he receives no relevant guidance in prison, presumably his female victims will be no safer when he is released.

The suggestion from all these areas of social casualty is that they stem from poor relations that both precipitate and follow other sorts of disturbance in people's behaviour that have previously been thought to be unconnected. A cure for the relationship disorders would help us on the way to curing the rest — a conviction that is increasingly shared by workers in a variety of helping professions.

Several of the foregoing are extreme examples, or concern only persistently poor relations. Unfortunately, everyday relationships also often go sour and repairing relationships that are seriously disturbed is not a simple job. It is one that is only becoming clearer through recent investigations, although its far-reaching consequences have been clarified more easily. There is now a growing awareness of the fact that there are two separate needs, each with different implications: the first need is for techniques to repair relationships; the second is for techniques to help people out of them and to help people get over them. In each case there are techniques for people to help themselves, techniques for them to help other people, and more formal techniques for intervention by counsellors and other agents of society.

The first crucial issue is one that echoes points made earlier. For people to be able to repair a breaking relationship they must be sure that they and their partner both desire the repair of the relationship. Research in USA recently has suggested that in normal relationships people tend to manage relationship distress by suppressing their feelings (Kaplan, 1976). They try to pretend that there is no problem. They expect that this will allow the problem to pass quietly, but it more often has undesired consequences. For instance it makes them angry, unconstructive, hostile and resentful. Instead most people, the research concludes, should bring their feelings out into the open: the discussion of the tensions in an accepting, constructive atmosphere can actually be helpful to the growth or repair of friendship (Kaplan, 1976).

When partners wish to stay in a relationship, as when they wish to leave or find themselves faced with a break up, the surrounding social network has an important influence on events (La Gaipa, 1982). By showing approval of a new partner, friend, date or fiancé, a person's friends, parents and kin can make it easier for the person to sustain the relationship in the knowledge that their judgement is accepted. When a relationship hits the rocks, the network can exert a similar cohesive force in one of two ways: first, and better, it can provide mediators and go-betweens who can encourage the parties to try to re-evaluate their own behaviours and to appreciate the perspective of the other person; second, and worse, it can exert social pressure upon people to bury and disguise their differences. In this latter case, the repair strategy would involve pointing out the person's obligations to their partner or to the social network, reinforcing the contractual nature of some institutional relationships (like marriage) and emphasising structural commitment to the relationship. If that is all that they do then the network will be successful only in plastering the couple together into a hollow and increasingly fragile shell of a relationship.

Effective strategies for repairing relationships depend on the stage of breakdown that has been reached (Duck, in press). If the relationship is merely turbulent and troubled, with resentment and hostility building up, then open expression of the reasons will help the two partners to decide what to do next. If things have gone further and partners are starting to feel dislike for one another, but wish to 'correct' it, then systematic focusing on the positive side of the partner and on the value of the relationship are useful strategies. Just writing out a list can help. If partners have felt so disaffected that they have withdrawn psychologically from the relationship then a reformulation of their expectancies about the relationship and a conscious change in behaviour and patterns of activity are necessary to effect repair. This may result in the relationship taking off again, or may cause the partners to prefer a new relationship with one another at a much lower level of intimacy (e.g. where lovers revert to being friends).

At this stage there is a fine balance between repairing the relationship by propping it up, and repairing the partners by extracting them gracefully from the relationship. In either case the network has a role. If the relationship is to be reformulated then the network has to be prepared to accept it in its new form, just as originally it had to accept it in its previous form. If the relationship is to be dismembered then the network has to assist if the dismemberment is to be widely accepted. Networks do this latter job by use of gossip and creation of stories or information that help everyone to see the relationship as unstable and unworthy of continuance. Such stories have been shown by Canadian research (La Gaipa, 1982) to involve the central theme that one or both partners has failed to live up to the socially-accepted friendship ideals (e.g. that the person failed to show ideal amounts of loyalty, confiding and trustworthiness, or failed to stand by the relationship in time of trouble). The network normally splits into two parts, one behind each partner as it supports that person's view of events. This story-writing is an essential feature of getting out of relationships. It is absolutely necessary for each partner and for the network as a whole to have a face-saving and acceptable public story about the ending of the relationship. Accordingly, one characteristic and under-estimated piece of behaviour is that people do a grave-dressing exercise after a relationship's death: that is, they tidy up the last resting place of the relationship, and present a neatly arranged story of how it all ended. Such stories are not only highly oversimplified (e.g. 'One day I just decided to get out'), but are often marked with elaborate grave-stones defining the partner as 'my dear departed ex' to emphasise the finality of it all. This fascinating aspect of relationships' endings has only just begun to receive attention, but is a vital part of the exercise of getting over a dead relationship. In counselling (both formal and informal) it is, therefore, an essential ingredient of the process and each partner must be encouraged to set up a story of how things went wrong. The more closely it can be made to accord with other people's stories the better. However it must be done one way or another, and is as essential a feature of getting out of a relationship as is the re-establishment of normal patterns of relationships afterwards.

The need to re-establish a normal pattern of relationships is a key one, too, and after divorce many people find this aspect of the business very depressing. When one loses a marriage partner one usually loses the friends that the partner brought to the marriage, and loyalties are often strained as between one partner's side of things and the other. Additionally, because people do not expect to be actively seeking new friends at the age when divorce occurs, they usually experience it as very threatening to have to do so, and the time that it takes can be painful.

For all of the reasons above, whether personal or circumstantial, the ending of relationships is a painful part of life. Unfortunately, it is one that we do not understand fully — for all its familiarity — and is one where positive research will help us to a better future for relationships.

Summary

In this chapter I have emphasised the many, many impersonal factors that can cause relationships to go wrong, such as changes in circumstances, and so on. I have stressed that, rather than looking only into their own souls for someone to blame, partners should consider the wider context of their problematic relationships and should give fullest thought to the range of circumstantial factors that can affect relationships — before they blame themselves. Length of time in relationship, time of year, the strategic approach of the two sexes to relationship, and in-effective styles of behaviour in general are all likely to influence a relationship's course, so the friendship can go wrong for all these unblameworthy reasons. Finally, I consider the role of the social network in the ending of relationships and the psych-ological importance of a credible 'public story' to explain the break. We need these public relations exercises every time a relationship falls apart. In all these considerations I emphasised the ways in which the future of friendship can be improved.

Epilogue: The Future of Friendship

People of every historical age have looked back and claimed that the past was the place where friendships were truly wonderful, and that present ones do not match up. Even in fourth-century BC Greece, Aristotle took the view that friendship had gone downhill since his grandfather's day!

The same tendency exists today. Everyone thinks that friendship (like the quality of life and beer) has deteriorated since the last century. The literature of that century and the previous one is often held up as evidence for this view, despite the general changes in social circumstances. We have all heard, too, the cliché that people nowadays are becoming 'alienated' as a consequence of an increasingly industrialised and technological society — that this has somehow spoiled the friendships and intricate dependencies that were possible in an essentially agricultural social system. We all decry the descent of friendship (even though no one has ever been able to put their finger on the sorts of tests and measurements that would be necessary to prove it), and we all look longingly to the past. Our age thus shares many of the disappointments and idealised hindsights of previous ages.

Uniquely, though, we are different. Of course, someone in a hundred years' time may indeed look back on the videotapes of the 1980s to show that, compared to the twenty-first century, our friendships are truly deep and significant. But it is the future of friendship that is going to be more satisfactory for the people who, in our own age, were merely stigmatised as social failures. I see a fundamental shift in attitudes to friendship (and to friendship deficiency) comparable to the shift in attitudes about the causes of illness that took place in the later middle ages. No

160

longer will lonely people be blamed as if they were merely sinners being punished by God, like physically sick people often used to be. They will be taught in childhood how to help themselves and if they need further help to perform properly in friendships, then it will be readily available without stigma.

Our descendants will come around to the view that incomplete friendship performance is not only personally distressing, but also socially harmful, and they will reject the simplistic idea which contends that lonely people have only themselves to blame. Simply blaming people does not help cure the problem and its social consequences. The lonely are not solely responsible for their 'deficiency', any more than children who cannot play the piano are solely to blame for theirs. By recognising that attitudes towards people and relationships are learned and shaped in childhood, we can also see that they can, like other types of learning, be improved by the use of proper techniques and proper education.

Improving Friendship

There are several things that I mean by 'improving friendship'. I have already drawn out many specific ideas, and I want to raise only general policy issues here. A major need is for the legitimation of difficulties with friendship and social relations as a problem that ought to be brought forward for discussion. For too long the stigma of failure has attached to poor relationships, and for too long this has encouraged people to take ways out of their difficulties which help them to disguise the true problem. When a person begins to feel the pain of loneliness it is presently more socially acceptable to take a few drinks, become depressed, or write to a problem page! There are no general and legitimated relationship clinics where people can take the problems to be dealt with openly and constructively. The nearest thing is the Samaritans — an excellent organisation, but one seen by many people as a port of last resort, rather than the sort of service that ought to be approached before then. Another kind of approach is provided by women's consciousness raising groups and encounter groups. These all help people to cope in various ways but often are the kinds of help sought rather late in the day. It is better to have this state of affairs than no help at all: but far better would be the creation of an atmosphere where people are less afraid to visit someone to discuss the problem. A beginning would be made with the recognition of the general extent of the problems and the growing resources available to resolve it. Once people can be encouraged to bring their relationship problems to legitimate resource centres, as they now take physical problems to a doctor, then they can turn to counselling programmes that can begin to play an effective role in reducing such social problems.

It is the knowledge of the far-reaching social consequences of friendship distress that makes the basis for such a plea. I have shown throughout this book the previously unforeseen and unrecognised consequences of friendship and its disturbance. I have also shown that the root cause lies not in some inherent and incurable unattractiveness of the persons involved but in the poor conduct of their relationships. Poor conduct, like poor health, poor diet or bad exercise programmes can be treated, and may be cured by the sorts of means indicated, whether by the person's own good sense or by formal intervention and guidance.

So-called loneliness intervention programmes have been begun in Canada and USA (e.g. Jones and Hansson, in preparation) and are a practical possibility even in England, as the Samaritans have indicated. Often it is just a case of people needing to talk in confidence about their relationships. However this useful first step is not in itself enough to do more than temporarily resolve the crisis. After this first step some extended and prolonged guidance about repairing relationships is probably necessary (for instance, in marriage breakdown) or some general changes in attitudes and behaviour towards other people (in the case of the chronically lonely person). It may even be necessary to make fundamental readjustments to a person's experiences of social attraction (for instance, in the case of distressed children or adolescents) and to prevent these poisoning the person's future life.

Loneliness intervention programmes have their first impact by being respectable and available. Their major value lies in the fact that distressed persons referred there do not regard themselves as anything more of a failure than someone does who catches 'flu and seeks medical advice. But a second value of legitimised loneliness intervention programme lies in their specific abilities to change lonely people's inappropriate friendship behaviour and to redirect ineffective attitudes about the person's own value and esteem. Of course it takes a lot of time to correct a complete set of attitudes about approaching and relating to other people, but the programmes in America have shown that it can be done, using the sort of ideas proposed in this book.

It is perhaps understandable that people find it very hard to accept that friendship does have such far-reaching social consequences, just as many people cannot bring themselves to accept that friendship can be improved by training. Yet we all believe that people work more effectively when they get on well, and that by careful personnel selection procedures we can put together effective work-teams. At the moment such selection is based largely on the intuition of personnel managers, or, in the case of dating agencies, on some of the early research work on similarity. It is only one step beyond this to employ the more recent and sophisticated techniques of later more advanced research and use them to create more effective and productive teams as well as happier and more stable and suitable marriages. For instance, since the productivity and effectiveness of a sales team is dependent on good relations between its members, it would make sense for managers and executives to use the friendship research on compatibility to help them select teams more effectively than by chance and intuitions. It goes deeper than mere selection of friendly people with similar values, and long-term deep similarities requires to be explored along with complementarities of behavioural styles. This is important less in selection of promising individuals than in selecting *sets* of promising individuals, since these do not necessarily make for effective teams that can get on well together. What is necessary is the selection of those promising individuals who can be predicted not only to like each other, but also to get on well in a productive and constructive way: i.e. who are complementary.

How is this possible? Research on friendship is always advancing and several research scientists now claim to have techniques that predict liking, many of which are based on compatibility studies using personality measures. The most effective are those that are not based on simple similarity but take account of the many different ways that personality can be measured and the different importance of the different aspects of personality that matter at different points in a growing relationship (Murstein, 1977). Although investigations are still proceedings, some researchers using such methods, can now predict much better than by chance whether two strangers will get on well — before they meet. These predictions also exceed those that are reliably successful by other means. The value of some of the long-term studies of friendship development has been in their indication of the changing influence of personality in liking over time as relationships grow, and some of the more sophisticated techniques put us within an ace of telling at first meeting who will get on well in what circumstances, and for how long. For instance, using one of these systems my research team was able to predict which of a set of students would be able to survive a year as flat-mates and which would not (Duck and Allison, 1978).

In relation to work productivity and other settings, however, the research has not yet been properly tested and many opportunities to develop good predictions of effective co-operation are being lost. But since we now know more not only about personality compatibility but, more importantly, about the ways in which people negotiate and create working relationships, the opportunities exist for practical exploitation of the research in the context of industrial work team selection. For example, it is now possible to match up apparently compatible pairs of people, to observe their acquaintance style in a brief exercise and thus predict their ultimate success in a particular type of relationship (Miell and Duck, 1982).

One step beyond that is the fact that the future of a marriage will soon be predictable by the advanced techniques currently being tested. Research teams in USA have now devised valid methods for charting the progress of courtships and classifying their main features as we have seen (Huston, *et al.*, 1981). Other workers have been tying this in with our knowledge about divorce, and it is only a matter of time before the two teams are able to show the relationship between courtship, the way a courtship is conducted, and the probability of eventual divorce. One ultimate use of such research is to develop these scientific procedures to the point where they can offer valid advice to engaged couples about the probable future of their marriage and the ways in which they must change in order to maximise its chances of survival. Marital therapy and marriage guidance is all very well once the marriage hits the rocks, but it is better for everyone if the rocks can be charted out before the journey begins. At present this is really all that people are doing when they have trial marriages of 'living together without the certificate' and again, they are merely being unscientific and intuitive. This is unsatisfactory, unreliable and full of room for improvement once more accurate techniques are freely available.

The future of friendship as well as marriage could also be tested in like manner now we are finding out so much more about how it works. We can now assess the likely compatibility of two people by means of scientific personality techniques, and, at the other end of the problem, my own research team has been looking at ways of making the most out of the basic compatibility that exists between two people. For instance, using theories about friendship development and structured acquainting methods we have been able to devise ways of helping people to find out about one another in great depth in a short time (Miell and Duck, 1982). Essentially, the technique is based on ideas given in chapter 3, and it involves the persons taking carefully selected areas of their own personality and talking about them with their partners. As experimenters we use advance pre-testing to ensure that partners will find that they are similar and compatible in these areas — hence the discussion will produce some attractive and rewarding discoveries, and the partners end up liking one another as well as feeling that they know each other well. If we merely left them to their own devices who knows whether they would ever pick up on the right areas to explore? They may even end up focusing on differences and end up disliking one another when a different strategy — a different sequence of discussions — can produce an opposite result. The sequence of discoveries is the important thing, we have found, and that further knocks on the head the idea that it is someone's characteristics or properties that make them attractive or unattractive to someone else. It isn't. It is the way and the order in which these are disclosed and discovered that counts.

However, these are not the only areas where such work on friendship is most significant — although it is important. From the point of view of its social value, the most important place to apply this research is in medicine. Medical research in the next twenty-five years will pay more attention to the strange connections between lack of friends and physical illness. Psychosomatic medicine has already explored the ways in which physical illness can result from mental states; it has also shown the effects on mental state that are caused by relationships and relationship problems. We are only just starting to find out that friendships are probably better than an apple a day at keeping us away from the doctor. But more than that, we are also finding out how friends can actually reinforce a doctor's influence on the patient by encouraging him to keep to prescribed advice, and so on.

I have mentioned many examples during the course of this book, so at this point I merely reiterate the serious fact that friendship distress can debilitate or even kill — and that most doctors do not yet treat it as if it does. More to the point, they usually treat the physical illness rather than the social one. More significant is the fact that treatment of the friendship problem is a more effective way to cure the patient's presented symptoms than is the usual application of drugs. The root problem — friendship disorder — is the basis for a wide variety of physical and psychological symptoms that can mislead even skilled diagnosticians.

Friendship and Social Policy

There are so many other issues in social life where friendship is important and where friendship research has useful advice that it is hard to know where to start. The most important issues concern children's learning of social relationships, the relationship consequences of unemployment, and several aspects of environmental or building designs. But there are also other issues where friendship research informs us usefully: it indicates lines of action in the treatment of violence towards women, the treatment of criminals, and hospital visiting hours. In all these cases it is a question of the experts who have done the research making it clear to other experts (e.g. architects or educators) what are the full implications and applications of their work for one another. Perhaps if this is done we can work together to avoid such social disasters as tower-block flats, and go some way to preventing the teenage delinquency that stems from poor relationships or misdirected group membership.

The major area for development here lies in the field of friendship education. There are presently no systematic attempts to deal with this necessary feature of our children's development into adulthood and this verges on the irresponsible. At present children and adolescents probably learn quite a bit from entering friendships that are doomed to failure, but the pain associated with such learning is still pain and it can last a long time. It could be reduced or prevented without removing the essential learning experience, if only schools would begin to take the learning of social relationships seriously. For instance, it is still common to find in children's storybooks and magazines the most extraordinary accounts of human friendships, just as there used to be vast amounts of hidden implications about racial differences (golliwogs, etc.) and sex differences that promoted views now thought to be unsatisfactory. Serious consideration of such things is truly a matter of social policy, in the manner that has been used in relation to sex discrimination and the undesired effects of portrayal of males and females in such places. So, too, is the issue of displaying and describing friendship in children's stories in a way that maximises a child's chance to learn theoretical lessons that can be practised in the playground. For instance, we need to be sure that the basis for friendship in children's stories is not portrayed at a level that they are not prepared for yet. We now know that it would be absurd to expect a 7-year-old to get anything from a friendship story describing trust, loyalty and secret-sharing — except they may get confused! This is not the basis for their own friendships, and it is no use telling them stories where it is shown to be one.

A more directly practical advance would be the bringing of friendship into the school curriculum. Merely encouraging children to write about it, think about it, play act it, and do projects on it can help them to become more aware of its importance and can help them in their development. A member of my research team has been doing just this and has tried out a number of ways of making children more sensitive to the nature of friendship (Brydon, 1982). He has used such techniques as a project where children mapped out their friendships and indicated by coloured pins and wire the relationship between friendship choices and housing position: in this way they are given a graphic picture of the influence of housing on friendship. Adolescents have also been encouraged to write essays and poems about friendship or even to act out relationships and then discuss them. Without fail they report this as a useful and valuable experience that helps them to come to terms with friendship. In these ways the children and adolescents are encouraged to think about friendship, to feel that it is a legitimate focus for their attention, and to see that it is a proper subject for public discussion. Furthermore, such methods would help the sensitive teacher or educational worker to spot potential social problems and nip them in the bud. Children with inefficient ideas about friendship or immaturity of approach to friendship behaviour could be more effectively identified and reserved for more intensive care and guidance.

Although childhood and adolescent friendships are the most pressing areas for making good use of the scientific research, there are other profitable avenues where it can be used. For instance, we have now found out a large amount about the friendship factors that influence satisfaction with buildings and living accommodation. The size of the community created by a building can be functional or dysfunctional, helpful or unhelpful. For example, in a communal residence the inhabitants prefer to have six people sharing a small kitchen than to have a larger community (say twenty-five) sharing a larger and better-equipped one. Also community feeling can be influenced by very minor building design points to do with location of post-boxes and lifts so as to lead to increased opportunity for meetings and for greater community atmosphere. Their purpose is not simply the literal one of accepting letters and elevating people: they have a social function, too. The most efficient arrangement of amenities from the building point of view may be the least acceptable from the social point of view. Research on friendship helps to show us how best to combine the two viewpoints.

A similar idea can be extended to such apparently purely administrative matters as the arrangement of visiting times in hospitals. It used to be thought that the visit itself was the desirable thing for the patient — and that times should be chosen on grounds of efficiency for hospital staff. Now the idea seems to be that patients should be allowed visitors whenever the visitors turn up, except for times that are maximally *in*efficient for the staff. (Incidentally, such times include the doctors round times. As evidence that scheduled and threatening visits can be fatal, let me add by the way that coronary patients have more attacks in the period just before consultants' rounds than at any other time during intensive care!) On the other hand, friendship researchers have shown convincingly that, from the patient's point of view, the most satisfactory relaxing and 'healing' arrangement is neither the tight schedule nor the random access system (Perlman and Peplau, 1981). The visits are most valuable and most satisfying for patients who can control arrangements themselves and when they know in advance when a visitor will come. Patients who could make up their own schedule of visits reported feeling better even if the visits were actually shorter or less frequent than those allowed to patients who had their visits scheduled for them. Given that time in hospitals is often extremely difficult for people, and that they benefit immeasurably from strong social support, we really ought to be more attentive to the friendship research in deciding about something so central to the patients as visiting arrangements. Proper thought about these alone can contribute substantially to recovery.

In addition to the implications of friendship research for educational policy, building design and hospital management, we should attend to a final area: the friendship implications of the growth in unemployment. As I showed earlier, many of a person's friendships are made at work — mostly because of the opportunity provided by meeting there. If opportunities for work continue to contract, and more people become unemployed, so they will lose these occasions for social contact and their friendships will fall into decay. We can expect, then, that loneliness, alcoholism and violence will increase sharply as a result. We can also see that families will be forced to spend more time together under one another's feet and that — as already happens during the extended public holidays particularly at Christmas — this will increase irritation with one another, and lead to increases in family disturbance or even divorce. A hidden cost of unemployment will thus emerge: social casualties from decreased friendships will begin to fall back more and more onto the state's rescue services. At present people are naïvely blaming such consequences on the loss of self-respect that follows redundancy. That is only part of it: the other part is a relationship problem.

What can be done? It will not be adequate merely to create unstructured opportunities for lonely people to meet (e.g. by building social centres), although this will help. Many people will be isolated by unemployment because at present there are probably many people who establish friendships only through work and only because the workplace structures their meetings with other people. The work thus subtly pushes them along in their friendships. Take away work and its structure, and you throw such people back on their own abilities to create relationships. Many people will need a great deal of help in such circumstances. The kinds of help required will be twofold: first, many people will need some sort of replacement structure for the relationships that the lost workplace used to make; second, many people will need the help of intervention programmes outlined earlier.

And so we come full circle, and conclude that the value of such programmes will be of inestimable value to our society in the years to come. Governments can set them up with ease once research on friendship begins to receive the deserved recognition for its potential. It is a practical study with far-ranging usefulness. It has already shown the vast number of apparently unrelated affairs into which friendships intrude, and where they can affect the conduct of life for good or ill. It promises to overturn even more of the cherished but unsupportable beliefs of common sense — and it holds out the possibility of genuine advances in the quality of life for a vast number of people. Whatever else happens in the next twenty-five years, it is clear that idle curiosity about friendship will be replaced by the more systematic knowledge accumulated by research into relationships and how they may be improved.

It is the only way to free us of the hidden 'relationship tax' that I mentioned in this book's opening sentences. Alas, whilst each of us pays 50p or $1 every day to settle the cost of the consequences of divorce, the sum we pay towards research that will help to stop it is presently pitifully small: it is 50 pence every sixty-seven years in the UK and, in USA about one dime every leap year.

Bibliography

Ajzen, I. (1977) 'Information processing approaches to inter-personal attraction', In Duck, S. W. (ed.), *Theory and Practice in Interpersonal Attraction*, Academic Press, London.

Argyle, M. (1969) *Social Interaction*, Methuen, London.

Argyle, M. (1978) *The Psychology of Interpersonal Behaviour* (3rd edn), Penguin, Harmondsworth.

Argyle, M., Furnham, A. and Graham, J. (1981) *Social Sit-*Psychology Section BPS Annual Conference, September, Oxford.

Argyle, M., Furnham, A. and Graham, J. (1981) *Social Situations*, Cambridge University Press, Cambridge.

Asher, S. R. and Gottman, J. (eds) (1981) *The Development of Children's Friendships*, Cambridge University Press, Cambridge.

Berscheid, E. and Walster, E. H. (1974) 'Physical attractive-ness' in *Advances in Experimental Social Psychology*, vol. 7, ed. L. Berkowitz, Academic Press, New York.

Bloom, B., Asher, S. and White, S. (1978) 'Marital disruption as a stressor: A review and analysis', *Psychological Bulletin 85*, 867-94.

Braiker, H. B. and Kelley, H. H. (1979) 'Conflict in the development of close relationships', in Burgess, R. L. and Huston, T. L. (eds), *Social Exchange in Developing Relationships*, Academic Press, New York.

Brydon, C. F. (1982) 'Children and adolescent friendships', Paper to Social Science Research Council Programme. Lancaster, July.

Bull, R. (1977) 'The psychological significance of facial dis-figurement', Paper to International Conference on Love and Attraction Swansea, Wales, September.

Burgess, R.L. (1981) 'Relationships in marriage and the family', in *Personal Relationships 1: Studying Personal Relationships*, ed. S.W. Duck and R. Gilmour, Academic Press, London.

Byrne, D. (1971) *The Attraction Paradigm*, Academic Press, New York.

Cate, R. and Christopher, F.S. (1982) 'Factors involved in premarital sexual decision making', Paper to International Conference on Personal Relationships, Madison Wisconsin, July.

Chelune, G.J. (1979) 'Measuring openness in interpersonal communcation', in Chelune, G.J. *et al.*, *Self Disclosure*, Jossey-Bass, London.

Chown, S.M. (1981) 'Friendship in old age', in *Personal Relationships 2: Developing Personal Relationships*, ed. S.W. Duck and R. Gilmour, Academic Press, London.

Collett, P. (1982) 'Meetings and misunderstandings', in *Cultures in Contact: Studies in cross-cultural interaction*, ed. S. Bochner, Pergamon, Oxford.

Cozby, P.C. (1973) 'Self Disclosure: A literature review', *Psychological Bulletin*, 79, 73-91.

Davis, J.D. (1978) 'When boy meets girl: sex roles and the negotiation of intimacy in an acquaintance exercise', *Journal of Personality and Social Psychology*, 36, 684-92.

Derlega, V.J. and Chaikin, A.L. (1976) 'Norms affecting self disclosure in men and women', *Journal of Consulting and Clinical Psychology*, 44, 376-80.

Dickens, W.J. and Perlman, D. (1981) 'Friendship over the life cycle', in *Personal Relationships 2: Developing Personal Relationships*, ed. S.W. Duck and R. Gilmour, Academic Press, London.

Di Matteo, R. (1979) 'A social psychological analysis of physician-patient rapport: Towards a science of the art of medicine', *Journal of Social Issues*, 35, 12-23.

Dion, K.K. and Berscheid, E. (1974) 'Physical attractiveness and peer perception among children', *Sociometry*, 37, 1-12.

Dion, K.L. and Dion, K.K. (1979) 'Personality and behavioural correlates of romantic love', in Cook, M. and Wilson, G. (eds) *Love and Attraction*, Pergamon, London.

Driscoll, R., Davis, K.E. and Lipetz, M.E. (1972) 'Parental interference and romantic love: The Romeo and Juliet effect', *Journal of Personality and Social Psychology*, 24, 1-10.

Duck, S.W. (1973a) 'Personality similarity and friendship

formation — similarity of what, when?' *Journal of Personality*, 41, 543-58.

Duck, S. W. (1973 b) *Personal Relationships and Personal Constructs, a study of friendship formation*, Wiley, London.

Duck, S. W. (1975) 'Personality similarity and friendship choices by adolescents', *European Journal of Social Psychology*, 5, 351-65.

Duck, S. W. (1977) *The Study of Acquaintance*, Teakfields, Saxon House, Farnborough.

Duck, S. W. (ed) (1982) *Personal Relationships 4: Dissolving Personal Relationships*, Academic Press, London.

Duck, S. W. (ed.) (in press) *Personal Relationships 5: Repairing Personal Relationships*. Academic Press, London.

Duck, S. W. and Allison, D. (1978) 'I liked you but I can't live with you: a study of lapsed friendships', *Social Behaviour and Personality*, 6, 43-7.

Duck, S. W. and Craig, G. (1978) 'Personality similarity and the development of friendship', *British Journal of Sociology and Clinical Psychology*, 17, 237-42.

Duck, S. W. and Gilmour, R. (eds) (1981 a) *Personal Relationships 1: Studying Personal Relationships*, Academic Press, London.

Duck, S. W. and Gilmour, R. (eds) (1981 b) *Personal Relationships 2: Developing Personal Relationships*, Academic Press, London.

Duck, S. W. and Gilmour, R. (eds) (1981 c) *Personal Relationships 3: Personal Relationships in Disorder*, Academic Press, New York.

Duck, S. W. and Lea, M. (1982) 'Breakdown of relationships as a threat to personal identity', in *Threatened Identities*, ed. G. Breakwell, Wiley, London.

Duck, S. W. and Miell, D. E. (1981) 'Charting the development of relationships', Paper to One Day Conference on Long-Term Relationships, Oxford, November.

Duck, S. W. and Miell, D. E. (1982) 'Toward an understanding of relationship development and breakdown', in *The Social Dimension: European Perspectives on Social Psychology*, ed. H. Tajfel, Cambridge University Press, Cambridge.

Festinger, L., Schachter, S. and Back, K. (1950) *Social Pressures in Informal Groups: A study of human factors in housing*, Harper & Row, New York.

Foot, H.C., Chapman, A.J. and Smith, J.R. (eds.) (1980) *Friendship and Social Relations in Children*, Wiley, London.

Frankel, A. and Morris, W.N. (1976) 'Testifying in one's own defense: the ingratiator's dilemma', *Journal of Personality and Social Psychology*, 34, 475-80.

Furman, W. (in preparation) 'Teaching relationship skills to unpopular children', in *Personal Relationships 5: Repairing Personal Relationships*, ed. S.W. Duck, Academic Press, London.

Gaebler, H.C. (1980) 'Children's friendships: The interaction of cognitive and social development', PhD thesis, University of Lancaster.

Guthrie, E.R. (1938) *The Psychology of Human Conflict*, Harper, New York.

Hagestad, G.O. and Smyer, M.A. (1982) 'Dissolving long-term relationships: Patterns of divorcing in middle age', in *Personal Relationships 4: Dissolving Personal Relationships,* ed. S.W. Duck, Academic Press, London.

Hatfield, E. and Traupmann, J. (1981) 'Intimate relationships: a perspective from equity theory, in *Personal Relationships 1: Studying Personal Relationships*, eds. S.W. Duck, and R. Gilmour, Academic Press, London.

Heider, F. (1958) *The Psychology of Interpersonal Relations*, Wiley, New York.

Hill, C.T., Rubin, Z. and Peplau, L.A. (1976) 'Breakups before marriage: The end of 103 affairs', *Journal of Social Issues*, 32, 147-68.

Hinde, R.A. (1979) *Towards Understanding Relationships*, Academic Press, London.

Hinde, R.A. (1981) 'The bases of a science of interpersonal relationships', in *Personal Relationships 1: Studying Personal Relationships*, eds. S.W. Duck and R. Gilmour, Academic Press, London, New York, San Francisco.

Howells, K. (1981) 'Social relationships in violent offenders', in *Personal Relationships 3: Personal Relationships in Disorder*, ed. S.W. Duck and R. Gilmour, Academic Press, London.

Huston, T., Surra, C., Fitzgerald, N. and Cate, R. (1981) 'From Courtship to marriage: Mate selection as an interpersonal process', in *Personal Relationships 2: Developing Personal Relationships*, ed. S.W. Duck and R. Gilmour, Academic Press, New York.

Johnson, M. (1982) 'Social and cognitive features of dissolving commitment to relationships', in *Personal Relationships 4 : Dissolving Personal Relationships*, ed. S. W. Duck, Academic Press, London.

Jones, E. E. and Gordon, E. M. (1972) 'Timing of self disclosure and its effects on personal attraction', *Journal of Personality and Social Psychology*, 24, 358-65.

Jones, W. and Hansson, R. (in preparation) 'Loneliness intervention programmes', in *Personal Relationships 5: Repairing Personal Relationships*, ed. S. W. Duck, Academic Press, London.

Jourard, S. M. (1971) *Self Disclosure*, Wiley, New York.

Kafer, N. (1981) 'Interpersonal strategies of unpopular children: some implications for social skill training', Paper to Lancaster University, Department of Psychology, November.

Kaplan, R. E. (1976) 'Maintaining interpersonal relationships: a bipolar theory, *Interpersonal Development*, 6, 106-19.

Kerckhoff, A. C. (1974) 'The social context of interpersonal attraction', in Huston, T. L., ed, *Foundations of Interpersonal Attraction*, Academic Press, New York.

Kon, I. S. (1981) 'Adolescent friendship: Some unanswered questions for future research', in *Personal Relationships 2 : Developing Personal Relationships*, ed. S. W. Duck and R. Gilmour, Academic Press, London.

La Gaipa, J. J. (1977) 'Interpersonal attraction and social exchange', in Duck, S. W. (ed.), *Theory and Practice in Interpersonal Attraction*, Academic Press, London.

La Gaipa, J. J. (1981) 'Children's friendships', in *Personal Relationships 2: Developing Personal Relationships*, ed. S. W. Duck and R. Gilmour, Academic Press, London.

La Gaipa, J. J. (1982) 'Rituals of disengagement', in *Personal Relationships 4: Dissolving Personal Relationships*, ed. S. W. Duck, Academic Press, London.

La Gaipa, J. J. and Wood, H. D. (1981) 'Friendship in disturbed adolescents', in Duck, S. W. and Gilmour, R. (ed), *Personal Relationships 3: Personal Relationships in Disorder*, Academic Press, London, New York.

Levinger, G. (1979) 'A social exchange view on the dissolution of pair relationships', in *Social Exchange in Developing Relationships*', ed. R. L. Burgess and T. L. Huston, Academic Press, New York.

Lynch, J.J. (1977) *The Broken Heart: The medical consequences of loneliness*, Basic Books, New York.

McCall, G. (1982) 'Becoming unrelated: the management of bond dissolution', in *Personal Relationships 4: Dissolving Personal Relationships*, ed. S. W. Duck, Academic Press, London.

McCarthy, B. (1981) 'Studying personal relationships', in *Personal Relationships 1: Studying Personal Relationships*, ed. S. W. Duck and R. Gilmour, Academic Press, London.

McCarthy, B. and Duck, S. W. (1976) 'Friendship duration and responses to attitudinal agreement-disagreement, *British Journal of Social and Clinical Psychology*, 15, 377-86.

Mangham, I. L. (1981) 'Relationships at work', in *Personal Relationships 1: Studying Personal Relationships*, ed. S. W. Duck and R. Gilmour, Academic Press, London.

Manning, M. and Herrmann, J. (1981) 'The relationships of problem children in nursery schools, in *Personal Relationships 3: Personal Relationships in Disorder*, ed. S. W. Duck and R. Gilmour, Academic Press, London.

Markman, H. J., Floyd, F. and Dickson-Markman, F. (1982) 'Towards a model for the prediction and primary prevention of marital and family distress and dissolution', in *Personal Relationships 4: Dissolving Personal Relationships*, ed. S. W. Duck, Academic Press, London.

Mehrabian, A. and Ksionzky, S. (1974) *A Theory of Affiliation*, Lexington Books, Lexington, Massachusetts.

Menges, R. J. (1969) 'Student-instructor cognitive compatibility in the large lecture class', *Journal of Personality*, 37, 444-59.

Miell, D. E. (in preparation) 'Self disclosure as strategic interaction', Paper in preparation, University of Lancaster.

Miell, D. E. and Duck, S. E. (1982) 'Similarity and acquaintance: The role of strategies', Paper to International Conference on Personal Relationships, Madison, Wisconsin, July.

Miell, D. E., Duck, S. W. and La Gaipa, J. J. (1979) 'Interactive effects of sex and timing of self disclosure', *British Journal of Social and Clinical Psychology*, 18 355-62.

Miller, G. R. and Parks, M. (1982) 'Communication in dissolving relationships', in *Personal Relationships 4: Dissolving Personal Relationships*, ed. S. W. Duck, Academic Press, London.

Morton, T. L. and Douglas, M. (1981) 'Growth of relationships', in *Personal Relationships 2: Developing Personal Relationships*, ed. S. W. Duck and R. Gilmour, Academic Press, London.

Murstein, B. I. (1977) 'The Stimulus-Value-Role (SVR) Theory of dyadic relationships', in *Theory and Practice in Interpersonal Attraction*, ed. S. W. Duck, Academic Press, London.

Newcomb, M. D. (1981) 'Heterosexual cohabitation relationships', in *Personal Relationships 1: Studying Personal Relationships*, ed. S. W. Duck and R. Gilmour, Academic Press, London, New York.

Newcomb, M. and Bentler, P. (1981) 'Marital breakdown', in *Personal Relationships 3: Personal Relationships in Disorder*, ed. S. W. Duck and R. Gilmour, Academic Press, New York.

Oden, S and Asher, S. R. (1977) 'Coaching children in social skills for friendship making, *Child Development* 48, 495-506.

Orford, J. (1980) 'The Domestic Context', in *Psychological Problems: The Social Context*, ed. M. P. Feldman and J. Orford, Wiley, Cambridge.

Orford, J. and O'Reilly, P. (1981) 'Disorders in the family', in *Personal Relationships 3: Personal Relationships in Disorder*, ed. S. W. Duck and R. Gilmour, Academic Press, London.

Peplau, L. A., Rubin, Z. and Hill, C. T. (1977) 'Sexual intimacy in dating relationships', *Journal of Social Issues*, 33, 86-109.

Perlman, D. and Peplau, L. A. (1981) 'Loneliness', in *Personal Relationships 3: Personal Relationships in Disorder*, ed. S. W. Duck and R. Gilmour, Academic Press, London.

Przybyla, D. and Byrne, D. (1981) 'Sexual relationships' in *Personal Relationships 1: Studying Personal Relationships,* ed. S. W. Duck and R. Gilmour, Academic Press, London.

Putallaz, M. and Gottman, J. M. (1981) 'Social skills and group acceptance', in *The Development of Children's Friendships*, ed. S. R. Asher and J. M. Gottman, Cambridge University Press, Cambridge.

Reis, H., Nezlek, J. and Wheeler, L. (1980) 'Physical attractiveness and social interaction, *Journal of Personality and Social Psychology*, 38, 604-17.

Reisman, J. (1981) 'Adult Friendships' in *Personal Relationships 2: Developing Personal Relationships*, ed S. W. Duck and R. Gilmour, Academic Press, London.

Rodin, M. (1982) 'Nonengagement, failure to engage and disengagement', in *Personal Relationships 4: Dissolving Personal Relationships*, ed. S. W. Duck, Academic Press, London.

Rubin, Z. (1974) 'From liking to loving: Patterns of attraction in dating relationships', in Huston, T. L. (ed), *Foundations of Interpersonal Attraction*, Academic Press, New York.

Rubin, Z. (1980) *Children's Friendships*, Harvard University Press, Cambridge, Massachussetts.

Schachter, S. (1959) *The Psychology of Affiliation*, Stanford University Press, Stanford, California.

Sherif, M. (1936) *The Psychology of Social Norms*, Harper & Row, New York.

Sigall, H. and Ostrove, N. (1975) 'Beautiful but dangerous: Effects of offender attractiveness and nature of crime on juridic judgement', *Journal of Personality and Social Psychology*, 31, 410-4-4.

Stroebe, W. (1977) 'Self esteem and interpersonal attraction', in *Theory and Practice in Interpersonal Attraction*, ed. S. W. Duck, Academic Press, London.

Takens, R. J. (1982) 'Psychotherapist-client relationships and effectiveness of therapy', Paper to International Conference on Personal Relationships, Madison, Wisconsin, July.

Thibaut, J. W. and Kelley, H. H. (1959) *The Social Psychology of Groups*, Wiley, New York.

Trower, P. (1981) 'Social skill disorder', in *Personal Relationships 3: Personal Relationships in Disorder*, ed. S. W. Duck and R. Gilmour, Academic Press, London.

Trower, P., Bryant, B. and Argyle, M. (1978) *Social Skills and Mental Health*, Methuen, London.

Walster, E., Walster, G. W. and Berscheid, E. (1978) *Equity Theory and Research*, Allyn & Bacon, Boston.

Weiss, R. S. (1974) 'The provisions of social relationships', in *'Doing Unto Others'*, ed. Z. Rubin, Prentice-Hall, New Jersey.

Wright, P. H. (1982) 'Developments of the Acquaintance Description Form', Paper to International Conference on Personal Relationships, Madison, Wisconsin, July.

Yaffe, M. (1981) 'Disordered sexual relationships', in *Personal Relationships 3: Personal Relationships in Disorder*, ed. S. W. Duck and R. Gilmour, Academic Press, London.

Index